KT-564-854

# Table of Contents

Copyright The Art of Service | Brisbane, Australia | Email: service@theartofservice.com
Web: http://theartofservice.com | eLearning: http://theartofservice.org | Phone: +61 (0)7 3252 2055

# 1 Operational Support and Analysis Functions

The term function in ITIL refers to the logical grouping of roles and automated measures that execute a defined process, an activity or combination of both. The functions involved with Operational Support & Analysis are required to enable the effective and efficient delivery and support of IT services. The functions are designed in such a way that aligned roles are grouped together so that it allows optimal application of resources, skills and knowledge of available staff. When using functions in this way, clear definition of roles and responsibilities is essential for developing a high performing and coordinated approach to Service Operation.

*"Know your role, do your job"*

*Team motto describing the goal for every player, coach and general staff member of the Kansas City Chiefs.*

Copyright The Art of Service | Brisbane, Australia | Email: service@theartofservice.com
Web: http://theartofservice.com | eLearning: http://theartofservice.org | Phone: +61 (0)7 3252 2055

WESTON COLLEGE

B70704

**Notice of Rights**

All rights reserved. No part of this book may be reproduced or transmitted in any form by any means, electronic, mechanical, photocopying, recording, or otherwise, without the prior written permission of the publisher.

**Notice of Liability**

The information in this book is distributed on an "As Is" basis without warranty. While every precaution has been taken in the preparation of the book, neither the author nor the publisher shall have any liability to any person or entity with respect to any loss or damage caused or alleged to be caused directly or indirectly by the instructions contained in this book or by the products described in it.

**Trademarks**

Many of the designations used by manufacturers and sellers to distinguish their products are claimed as trademarks. Where those designations appear in this book, and the publisher was aware of a trademark claim, the designations appear as requested by the owner of the trademark. All other product names and services identified throughout this book are used in editorial fashion only and for the benefit of such companies with no intention of infringement of the trademark. No such use, or the use of any trade name, is intended to convey endorsement or other affiliation with this book.

**Write a review to receive any *free* eBook from our Catalog - $99 Value!**

If you recently bought this book we would love to hear from you! Benefit from receiving a free eBook from our catalog at http://www.emereo.org/ if you write a review on Amazon (or the online store where you purchased this book) about your last purchase!

**How does it work?**

To post a review on Amazon, just log in to your account and click on the Create your own review button (under Customer Reviews) of the relevant product page. You can find examples of product reviews in Amazon. If you purchased from another online store, simply follow their procedures.

**What happens when I submit my review?**

Once you have submitted your review, send us an email at review@emereo.org with the link to your review, and the eBook you would like as our thank you from http://www.emereo.org/. Pick any book you like from the catalog, up to $99 RRP. You will receive an email with your eBook as download link. It is that simple!

Copyright The Art of Service │ Brisbane, Australia│ Email: service@theartofservice.com
Web: http://theartofservice.com │ eLearning: http://theartofservice.org │ Phone: +61 (0)7 3252 2055

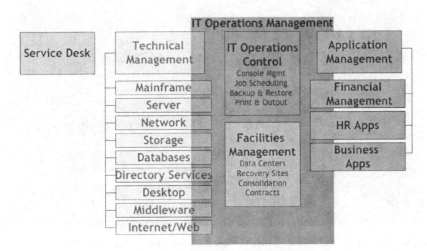

**The ITIL® Functions from Service Operation**

**NOTE:** These are logical functions and do not necessarily have to be performed by equivalent organizational structure. This means that Technical and Application Management can be organized in any combination and into any number of departments. The lower groupings (e.g. Mainframe, Server) are examples of activities performed by Technical Management and are not a suggested organizational structure.

## 1.1 The Service Desk

A Service Desk is a functional unit that acts as the primary point (first line) of contact for the end user community for all incidents, requests and general communication that arise. It plays an essential and valuable role for any organization, contributing significantly to the satisfaction of users and the overall impression of the IT organization. Depending on the type of business, services and technology supported, the exact size and physical organization of the Service Desk will vary from a small centralized team to a diverse range of teams in multiple locations and time zones.

Copyright The Art of Service | Brisbane, Australia | Email: service@theartofservice.com
Web: http://theartofservice.com | eLearning: http://theartofservice.org | Phone: +61 (0)7 3252 2055

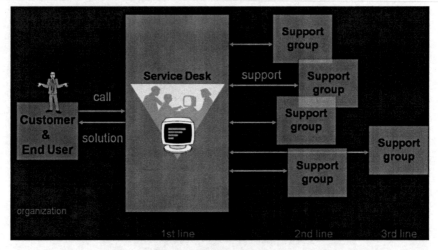

**The Service Desk acting a 'Single Point of Contact' for the end user community**

## Goal and objectives

The primary goal of the Service Desk is to support the agreed IT service provision by ensuring the accessibility and availability of the IT-organization and by performing various supporting activities. Other objectives include:

- To act as a single point of contact for all user incidents, requests and general communication
- To restore 'normal service operation' as quickly as possible in the case of disruption
- To improve user awareness of IT issues and to promote appropriate use of IT services and resources
- To assist other the other IT functions by managing user communication and escalating incidents and requests using defined procedures.

Copyright The Art of Service | Brisbane, Australia | Email: service@theartofservice.com
Web: http://theartofservice.com | eLearning: http://theartofservice.org | Phone: +61 (0)7 3252 2055

## Benefits

While many organizations have already seen the justification for the creation of a Service Desk team(s), in many cases the business case for the improvement fail to gain support from various levels of management. As discussed earlier, the needs and requirements will vary significantly for each organization, however the typical benefits gained through the implementation/improvement of a Service Desk function includes:

- Improved customer service perception, and satisfaction
- Increased accessibility through the use of a single point of contact
- Better quality and speedier turnaround of requests
- Improved teamwork and communication
- Better managed infrastructure and control
- Improved usage of IT resources.

Copyright The Art of Service | Brisbane, Australia | Email: service@theartofservice.com
Web: http://theartofservice.com | eLearning: http://theartofservice.org | Phone: +61 (0)7 3252 2055

# Service Desk organizational structures

Many factors will influence the way in which a Service Desk function will be physically structured, such as the location, languages and cultures of end users, diversity in services and technology supported and the objectives governing the implementation of the Service Desk such as improved satisfaction or reduced operating costs.

The following is some of the main options chosen when implementing a Service Desk function:

### Local Service Desk

A local Service Desk structure is where the Service Desk is co-located within or physically close to the user community it serves. This may aid in communication and give the Service Desk a visible presence which some users may like. It may however be inefficient and expensive as a result of having multiple Service Desks operating.

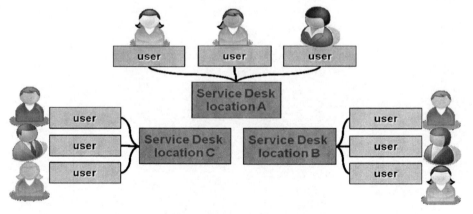

**The local Service Desk structure**

Copyright The Art of Service | Brisbane, Australia | Email: service@theartofservice.com
Web: http://theartofservice.com | eLearning: http://theartofservice.org | Phone: +61 (0)7 3252 2055

| Benefits of a Local Service Desk structure | Disadvantages of a Local Service Desk structure |
| --- | --- |
| • Local and specific user knowledge<br>• Ability to effectively communicate with multiple languages<br>• Appropriate cultural knowledge<br>• Visible (and physical) presence of the Service Desk | • Higher costs for replicated infrastructure and more staff involved<br>• Less knowledge transfer, each Service Desk may spend time rediscovering knowledge.<br>• Inconsistency in service levels and reporting<br>• Service Desks may be focused on local issues |

*Centralized Service Desk*

A centralized structure uses a Service Desk in a single location (or smaller number of locations), although some local presence may remain to handle physical support requirements such as deploying, moving and disposing of user workstations. This could be more efficient, enabling less staff to manage a higher volume of calls, with greater visibility of repeat incidents and request.

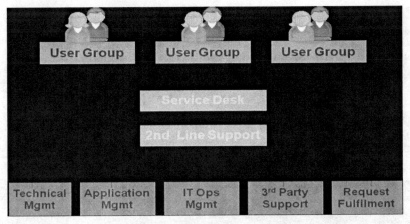

**The centralized Service Desk structure**

Copyright The Art of Service | Brisbane, Australia | Email: service@theartofservice.com
Web: http://theartofservice.com | eLearning: http://theartofservice.org | Phone: +61 (0)7 3252 2055

| Benefits of a centralized Service Desk structure | Disadvantages of a centralized Service Desk structure |
|---|---|
| • Reduced operational costs<br>• Improved usage of available resources<br>• Consistency of call handling<br>• Improved ability for knowledge sharing<br>• Simplicity for users (call one number) to contact the Service Desk | • Potentially higher costs and challenges in handling 24x7 environment or different time zone<br>• Lack of local knowledge<br>• Possible gaps in language and culture<br>• Higher risk (single point of failure), in case of power loss or other physical threat. |

### Virtual Service Desk

A Virtual Service Desk through the use of technology, particularly the Internet and the use of corporate support tools, can give users the impression of a single, centralized Service Desk when in fact the personnel may be spread or located in any number or type of geographical or structural locations.

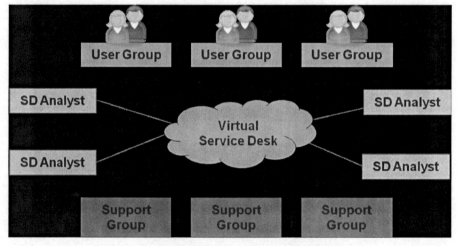

**A virtual Service Desk structure**

Copyright The Art of Service │ Brisbane, Australia │ Email: service@theartofservice.com
Web: http://theartofservice.com │ eLearning: http://theartofservice.org │ Phone: +61 (0)7 3252 2055

| Benefits of a virtual Service Desk structure | Disadvantages of a virtual Service Desk structure |
|---|---|
| • Support for global organizations<br>• 24x7 support in multiple time zones<br>• Reduced operational costs<br>• Improved usage of available resources<br>• Effective matching of appropriate staff for different types of calls | • Initial cost of implementation, requiring diverse and effective voice technology<br>• Lack in the consistency of service and reporting<br>• Less effective for monitoring actions of staff<br>• Staff may feel disconnected from other Service Desk staff |

Copyright The Art of Service | Brisbane, Australia | Email: service@theartofservice.com
Web: http://theartofservice.com | eLearning: http://theartofservice.org | Phone: +61 (0)7 3252 2055

## *Follow the Sun*

Some global or international organizations will combine two or more of their geographically dispersed Service Desks to provide 24-hour follow-the-sun service.

**A 'Follow the Sun' Service Desk structure**

| Benefits of a 'Follow the Sun' Service Desk structure | Disadvantages of a 'Follow the Sun' Service Desk structure |
|---|---|
| <ul><li>Support for global organizations</li><li>24x7 support in multiple time zones</li><li>Improved quality of service</li><li>Improved customer/user satisfaction</li><li>Effective knowledge sharing and high level visibility of distributed infrastructure</li></ul> | <ul><li>Typically higher operating costs</li><li>Cost of required technology</li><li>Challenges in using single language for multiple regions when recording knowledge, workarounds, Known Errors etc</li></ul> |

Copyright The Art of Service │ Brisbane, Australia │ Email: service@theartofservice.com
Web: http://theartofservice.com │ eLearning: http://theartofservice.org │ Phone: +61 (0)7 3252 2055

# Service Desk Types (skill levels)

Depending on the requirements defined for the Service Desk, organizations will need to consider what skill level is appropriate for the Service Desk and the support it will offer. This skill level can be defined in many ways, but most often is associated with the first time resolution achieved for calls, incidents and requests made to the Service Desk by users.

**The 3 types of Service Desks are:**

- **Call Centre:** Responsible for *handling/logging* of large volumes of calls
- **Help Desk:** Responsible for **managing** and *co-ordinate* incidents
- **Service Desk:** Responsible for **managing** incidents and requests, and also provides a wide variety supporting services (e.g. supporting Human Resources)

**Relationship between Service Desk types, costs and first-time resolution**

Copyright The Art of Service | Brisbane, Australia | Email: service@theartofservice.com
Web: http://theartofservice.com | eLearning: http://theartofservice.org | Phone: +61 (0)7 3252 2055

## Service Desk staffing

One of the most challenging issues facing a Service Desk Manager is that of staffing, with many organizations finding it increasingly difficult to acquire and retain quality employees. Additionally, determining appropriate staff levels can be difficult, with call rates being very volatile and dynamic. The following section will describe some of the issues involved with staffing a Service Desk.

### *Hiring Service Desk staff*

Most Service Desk Managers will have a list of key competencies or selection criteria that is used when hiring new staff members. Depending on the type of Service Desk that has been implemented and what types of technologies are being supported these criteria will vary, however typical skills required include:
- Communication skills
- Technical knowledge
- Business understanding
- Diagnosis and analysis skills
- Understanding of the role/value of processes and procedures
- Typing skills.

Communication skills are ultimately the most important as they will need to be able to deal effectively with a wide-range of people and stressful situations.

Copyright The Art of Service | Brisbane, Australia | Email: service@theartofservice.com
Web: http://theartofservice.com | eLearning: http://theartofservice.org | Phone: +61 (0)7 3252 2055

## Service Desk staffing levels

The number of staff employed on the Service Desk is dependent on the needs of the business, the objectives/goals defined and a range of other important criteria including:

- Business budget
- Customer service expectations
- Size, maturity, design, complexity of the IT Infrastructure & service catalog
- The number of customers and users to support
- The volume of requests, incidents and general communication required
- Period of support cover required
- Workload pattern of requests
- SLA definitions in place
- Level of training required
- Support technologies available.

## Super Users

'Super Users' are often useful positions to be appointed across an organization to act as liaison points with the IT organization and the Service Desk in particular. Super Users can be used in a number of ways such as:

- To assist in general communication between the Service Desk and users
- To filter requests and issues raised by the user community
- To assist in user training.

While Super Users can be a valuable resource if they are properly coordinated, the following rules should be in place:

- Roles and responsibilities are clearly defined
    - Escalation channels are defined

Copyright The Art of Service | Brisbane, Australia | Email: service@theartofservice.com
Web: http://theartofservice.com | eLearning: http://theartofservice.org | Phone: +61 (0)7 3252 2055

- Standard support processes defined and used
- All requests recorded and maintained consistently.

## *Staff retention*

To ensure a balanced mix of experienced and newer staff, Service Desk Managers should use a number of methods and incentives to retain quality staff and to avoid disruption and inconsistency in the quality of support offered.

Some ways in which this can be done include:
- Recognition of staff achievements contributing to service quality
- Rotation of staff onto other activities (projects, second-line support etc.)
- Team building exercises and celebrations
- Promote the Service Desk as a potential stepping stone for staff to move into other more technical or supervisory roles (after defined time periods and skills achieved).

Copyright The Art of Service | Brisbane, Australia | Email: service@theartofservice.com
Web: http://theartofservice.com | eLearning: http://theartofservice.org | Phone: +61 (0)7 3252 2055

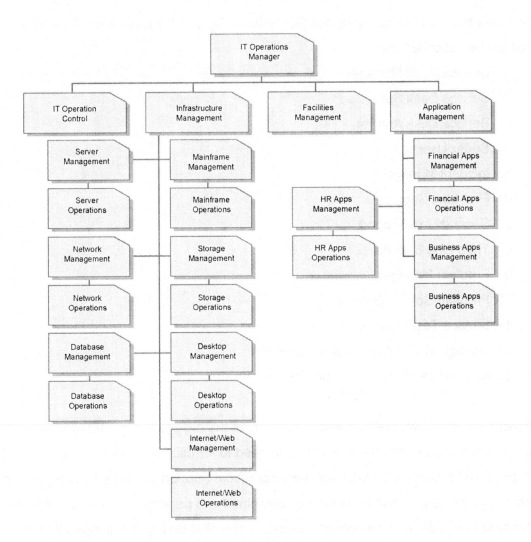

**Example of an organizational structure for Service Operation**

© Crown Copyright 2007 Reproduced under license from OGC

Copyright The Art of Service | Brisbane, Australia | Email: service@theartofservice.com
Web: http://theartofservice.com | eLearning: http://theartofservice.org | Phone: +61 (0)7 3252 2055

The roles required for managing the Operational Support & Analysis for IT Services that will be described are:

1.  Service Desk Manager
2.  Service Desk Supervisor
3.  Service Desk Analyst
4.  Super User
5.  Incident Manager
6.  First Line Support
7.  Second Line Support
8.  Third Line Support
9.  Problem Manager
10. Problem-Solving Groups
11. Service Test Manager
12. Configuration Administrator/Librarian
13. Knowledge Management process owner.

Depending on the relative size and complexity of the organizations, and requirements for service management, there may be the need to formally define extra roles responsible for specific elements of the Operational Support & Analysis processes. In other organizations, these roles may be combined and performed by one individual. Regardless of size, all organizations should ensure that testing is managed and performed by resources independent of other functions and processes.

## 1. Service Desk Manager

In large organizations where the Service Desk is of a significant size, a Service Desk Manager role may be justified with the Service Desk Supervisor(s) reporting to him or her. In such cases this role may take responsibility for some of the activities listed above and may additionally perform the following activities:

- Manage the overall desk activities, including the supervisors

Copyright The Art of Service | Brisbane, Australia | Email: service@theartofservice.com
Web: http://theartofservice.com | eLearning: http://theartofservice.org | Phone: +61 (0)7 3252 2055

- Act as a further escalation point for the supervisor(s)
- Take on a wider customer-services role
- Report to senior managers on any issue that could significantly impact the business
- Attend Change Advisory Board meetings
- Take overall responsibility for incident and Service Request handling on the Service Desk. This could also be expanded to any other activity taken on by the Service Desk – e.g. monitoring certain classes of event.

Note: in all cases, clearly defined job descriptions should be drafted and agreed so that specific responsibilities are known.

## 2. Service Desk Supervisor

In very small desks it is possible that the senior Service Desk Analyst will also act as the Supervisor – but in larger desks it is likely that a dedicated Service Desk Supervisor role will be needed. Where shift hours dictate it, there may be two or more post-holders who fulfill the role, usually on an overlapping basis. The Supervisor's role is likely to include:

- Ensuring that staffing and skill levels are maintained throughout operational hours by managing shift staffing schedules, etc.
- Undertaking HR activities as needed
- Acting as an escalation point where difficult or controversial calls are received
- Production of statistics and management reports
- Representing the Service Desk at meetings
- Arranging staff training and awareness sessions
- Liaising with senior management
- Liaising with Change Management
- Performing briefings to Service Desk staff on changes or deployments that may

Copyright The Art of Service | Brisbane, Australia | Email: service@theartofservice.com
Web: http://theartofservice.com | eLearning: http://theartofservice.org | Phone: +61 (0)7 3252 2055

affect volumes at the Service Desk

- Assisting analysts in providing first-line support when workloads are high, or where additional experience is required.

## 3. Service Desk Analysts

The primary Service Desk Analyst role is that of providing first-level support through taking calls and handling the resulting incidents or Service Requests using the Incident Reporting and Request Fulfillment processes, in line with the Service Desk objectives.

## 4. Super Users

In summary, this role will consist of business users who act as liaison points with IT in general and the Service Desk in particular. The role of Super User can be summarized as follows:

- To facilitate communication between IT and the business at an operational level
- To reinforce expectations of users regarding what Service Levels have been agreed
- Staff training for users in their area
- Providing support for minor incidents or simple request fulfillment
- Involvement with new releases and rollouts.

## 5. Incident Manager

An Incident Manager has the responsibility for:

- Driving the efficiency and effectiveness of the Incident Management process.
- Producing management information
- Managing the work of incident support staff (first and second-line)
- Monitoring the effectiveness of Incident Management and making

Copyright The Art of Service | Brisbane, Australia | Email: service@theartofservice.com
Web: http://theartofservice.com | eLearning: http://theartofservice.org | Phone: +61 (0)7 3252 2055

recommendations for improvement

- Developing and maintaining the Incident Management systems
- Managing Major Incident
- Developing and maintaining the Incident Management process and procedures.

In many organizations the role of the Incident Manager is assigned to the Service Desk Supervisor – through in larger organizations with high volumes a separate role may be necessary. In either case it is important that the Incidents effectively through first, second and third line.

## 6. First Line Support

The Service Desk is the primary point of contact for users when there is a service disruption, for service requests or even for some categories of Request for Change. The Service Desk provides a point of communication to the users and a point of coordination for several IT groups and processes. To enable them to perform these actions effectively the Service Desk is usually separate from the other Service Operation functions. In some cases, e.g. where detailed technical support is offered to users on the first call, it may be necessary for Technical or Application Management staff to be on the Service Desk. This does not mean that the Service Desk becomes part of the Technical Management function. In fact, while they are on the Service Desk, they cease to be a part of the Service Desk, even if only temporarily.

## 7. Second Line Support

Many organizations will choose to have a second-line support group, made up of staff with greater (though still general) technical skills than the Service Desk – and with additional time to devote to incident diagnosis and resolution without interference from telephone interruptions. Such a group can handle many of the less complicated

21

Copyright The Art of Service | Brisbane, Australia| Email: service@theartofservice.com
Web: http://theartofservice.com | eLearning: http://theartofservice.org | Phone: +61 (0)7 3252 2055

incidents, leaving more specialist (third-line) support groups to concentrate on dealing with more deep-rooted incidents and/or new developments etc.

Where a second-line group is used, there are often advantages of locating this group close to the Service Desk to aid with communications and to ease movement of staff between the groups, which may be helpful for training/awareness and during busy periods of staff shortages. A second-line support manager (or supervisor if just a small group) will normally head this group.

It is conceivable that this group may be outsourced – and this is more likely and practical if the Service Desk itself has been outsourced.

## 8. Third Line Support

Third – line support will be provided by a number of internal technical groups and/or third-party suppliers/maintainers. The list will vary from organization to organization but is likely to include:

- Network Support
- Voice Support
- Server Support
- Desktop Support
- Application Management – likely that there may be separate teams for different applications or application types – some of which may be external supplier/maintainers. In many cases the same team will be responsible for Application Development as well as support – and it is therefore important that resources are prioritized so that support is given adequate prominence
- Database Support
- Hardware Maintenance Engineers
- Environment Equipment Maintainers/Suppliers.

Copyright The Art of Service | Brisbane, Australia | Email: service@theartofservice.com
Web: http://theartofservice.com | eLearning: http://theartofservice.org | Phone: +61 (0)7 3252 2055

**Note**: Depending upon where an organization decides to source its support services, any of the above groups could be internal or external groups.

## Key Performance Indicators (KPIs) for the Service Desk

To evaluate the true performance of the Service Desk, a balanced range of metrics should be established and reviewed at regular intervals. Especially dangerous is the tendency to focus on "average call time" or "number of calls answered" metrics which can mask underlying issues with the quality of support provided.

Some of the typical metrics reviewed when monitoring the performance of the Service Desk include:
 The number of calls to Service Desk (broken down by type, time of day and day of the week)

- First-line resolution rate
- Average Service Desk cost of handling any incident or request
- Number of knowledgebase articles created
- Number or percentage of SLA breaches
- Call resolution time
- Customer satisfaction (surveys)
- Use of self help (where exists).

## Outsourcing the Service Desk

Although fairly common, there are potential risks that can be introduced when outsourcing an organization's Service Desk. When reviewing the potential for this to occur, Service Managers should consider the following items when developing contracts to reduce these risks:

- Use of your own Service Management tool, not theirs
  - Retain ownership of data

23

- Ability to maintain required staffing levels
- Agreements on reporting and monitoring needs
- Proven up to date procedures
- Agreed and understood support needs
- Engage contract specialists for assistance.

## 1.2 Technical Management

To enable regular Service Operation, one or more technical support teams or departments will be required to provide Technical Management and support for the IT Infrastructure. In all but the smallest organizations where a single combined team or department may suffice, separate teams or departments will be needed for each type of infrastructure being used. In many organizations the Technical Management departments are also responsible for the daily operation of a subset of the IT Infrastructure.

Technical Management plays an important role within Operational Support & Analysis by:
- Being the custodian of technical knowledge and expertise related to managing the IT Infrastructure
- Providing detailed technical skills and resources needed to support the ongoing operation of the IT Infrastructure
- Providing the actual resources to support the IT Service Management lifecycle
- Ensuring resources are effectively trained and deployed to design, build, transition, operate and improve the technology to deliver and support IT Services.

Copyright The Art of Service | Brisbane, Australia | Email: service@theartofservice.com
Web: http://theartofservice.com | eLearning: http://theartofservice.org | Phone: +61 (0)7 3252 2055

| Technical Management |
|---|
| Mainframe |
| Server |
| Network |
| Storage |
| Databases |
| Directory Services |
| Desktop |
| Middleware |
| Internet/Web |

Technical Management is usually organized into teams or departments dealing with technology areas such as:

- Mainframes
- Servers
- Storage devices
- Networks
- Desktops and Standard Operating Environments
- Databases
- Middleware
- Directory Services
- Messaging
- Telecommunications (including VOIP).

## Goal and Objectives

The Technical Management function's primary goal is to plan, implement and maintain a stable technical infrastructure that supports the organization's business processes.

This is achieved through:

- Well designed, highly resilient, cost effective technical architectures
- The use of adequate technical skills to maintain the technical infrastructure in optimum condition
- Swift use of technical skills to speedily diagnose and resolve any technical failures that do occur.

Copyright The Art of Service | Brisbane, Australia | Email: service@theartofservice.com
Web: http://theartofservice.com | eLearning: http://theartofservice.org | Phone: +61 (0)7 3252 2055

Technical
Management

**Specialist Technical
Architects & Designers**

*(Primarily involved in Service
Design)*

**Specialist Maintenance
& Support Staff**

*(Primarily involved in
Service Operation)*

**Involvement of Technical Management within the Service Lifecycle**

To enable quality knowledge sharing and continual improvement of services, technology, processes and other capabilities, Technical Management staff should develop effective communication channels and meet regularly to discuss issues or potential ideas. History demonstrates that quality design requires involvement from those who will be supporting the product/service, as does quality support require involvement from the designers in turn.

## Key Performance Indicators (KPIs) for Technical Management

The metrics chosen to evaluate the performance of Technology Management will largely depend on which technology is being managed, however some generic metrics areas include:

- Measurement of agreed outputs
    - Contribution in support/enhancement of business processes
    - Knowledge transferred to other teams and functions
    - Training provided
    - Availability of key infrastructure provided
    - Transaction rates supported
    - Installation and configuration of CIs under their control
- Process metrics
    - Number of events captured and managed (grouped by type)

Copyright The Art of Service | Brisbane, Australia | Email: service@theartofservice.com
Web: http://theartofservice.com | eLearning: http://theartofservice.org | Phone: +61 (0)7 3252 2055

- o Resolution timeframes for escalated incidents and problems
- o Number of changes implemented and backed out
- o Costs incurred against those budgeted
- o Security issues detected and resolved
- o SLA compliance/exceptions
- Technology performance
  - o Capacity provided
  - o Utilization rates
  - o Availability of services and systems
  - o Individual CI performance rates
- Mean time between failures of specified equipment
  - o Percentage of purchased components that remain in place for length of time as expected
- Measurement of maintenance activity
- Training and skills development.

## 1.3  IT Operations Management

IT Operations Management is the function that provides capabilities for performing the daily operational activities required to maintain a stable production (live) environment. In many ways, the function performs many of the logistical activities required for the effective and efficient delivery and support of services (e.g. Event Management).

It is shown in the figure below with an overlap to the Technical Management and Application Management functions, as many of the activities performed will involve elements of the technical infrastructure or applications being supported. In some organizations this means that many of the IT Operations Management activities are performed by the other functions themselves, but in larger organizations it is more common that a centralized group of staff will be designated with responsibility. Good

Copyright The Art of Service | Brisbane, Australia | Email: service@theartofservice.com
Web: http://theartofservice.com | eLearning: http://theartofservice.org | Phone: +61 (0)7 3252 2055

practice generally recommends that Technical and Application Management areas should manage new and unstable systems and applications, and transfer them to IT Operations Management when they have matured.

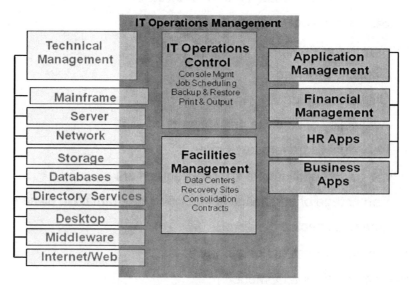

**IT Operations Management**

## Goal and objectives

The primary goal of IT Operations Management is to perform the IT organization's day to day operational activities using repeatable and consistent actions. Some of the objectives include:

- Maintenance of the 'status quo' to achieve stability of the organization's day to day processes and activities
- Regular scrutiny and improvements to achieve improved service at reduced costs, whilst maintaining stability
- Swift application of operational skills to diagnose and resolve any IT operations failures that occur.

Copyright The Art of Service | Brisbane, Australia | Email: service@theartofservice.com
Web: http://theartofservice.com | eLearning: http://theartofservice.org | Phone: +61 (0)7 3252 2055

## Operations Control

One role played by IT Operations Management is that of Operations Control. This role is concerned with the execution and monitoring of the operational activities and events in the IT infrastructure (possibly using an Operations/Network Bridge). In addition to the routine tasks to be performed in accordance with the design specifications of the IT infrastructure, Operations Control is also responsible for the following:

- Monitoring and Control
- Console Management
- Job Scheduling
- Backup and restores
- Print and Output Management

Copyright The Art of Service | Brisbane, Australia | Email: service@theartofservice.com
Web: http://theartofservice.com | eLearning: http://theartofservice.org | Phone: +61 (0)7 3252 2055

## 1.4 Technology Considerations

Technology is a significant factor in the quality and success of Operational Support & Analysis for the modern service provider. The two main ways in which delivery and support of services is supported by technology are:

- Enterprise-wide tools that support the broader systems and processes within which support is delivered.
- Tools targeted more specifically at supporting Service Operation.

The following systems support the wider scope for enterprise requirements, providing automated support for some elements of Service Operation:

- IT Service Management systems:
    - Enterprise frameworks
    - System, network and applications management tools
    - Service dashboards and reporting tools.
- Specific ITSM technology and tools that cover:
    - SKMS
    - Collaborative, content management, workflow tools
    - Data mining tools
    - Extract, load and transform data tools
    - Measurement and reporting systems
    - Test Management and testing tools
    - Database and test data management tools
    - Copying and publishing tools
    - Release and deployment technology
    - Deployment and logistics systems and tools.

With particular focus on the Service Operation processes, tools and systems that can

Copyright The Art of Service │ Brisbane, Australia│ Email: service@theartofservice.com
Web: http://theartofservice.com │ eLearning: http://theartofservice.org │ Phone: +61 (0)7 3252 2055

be utilized include:

- Configuration Management Systems (CMS) and tools
- Monitoring Agents and Event Correlation Engines
- Databases for the storage of Incident, Problem and Known Error Records
- Discovery tools
- Virtualization for simulating multiple environments
- Detection and recovery tools
- Backup and recovery tools.

While the needs for supporting technology will be influenced by a large number of factors, an integrated suite of ITSM tools and systems should generally include the following functionality:

- Self-help
- Workflow or process engine
- Integrated CMS
- Discovery/Deployment/Licensing technology
- Remote control
- Diagnostic utilities
- Reporting
- Dashboards
- Integration with Business Service Management.

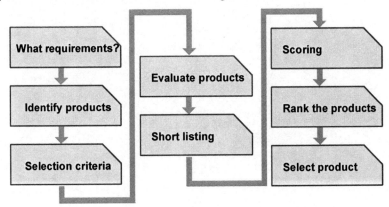

Copyright The Art of Service | Brisbane, Australia | Email: service@theartofservice.com
Web: http://theartofservice.com | eLearning: http://theartofservice.org | Phone: +61 (0)7 3252 2055

© Crown Copyright 2007 Reproduced under license from OGC

Typical items to consider when evaluating various products for the most appropriate selection include:

- Data structure
- Integration
- Conformity
- Flexibility
- Usability
- Support for monitoring service levels
- Conversion requirements
- Support options
- Scalability
- Tool and Vendor credibility
- Training needs
- Customization
- What level of adaptation is needed to implement the product successfully?

Copyright The Art of Service | Brisbane, Australia | Email: service@theartofservice.com
Web: http://theartofservice.com | eLearning: http://theartofservice.org | Phone: +61 (0)7 3252 2055

# 2 Supporting documents

**Through the documents, look for text surrounded by << and >> these are indicators for you to create some specific text.**

Copyright The Art of Service | Brisbane, Australia | Email: service@theartofservice.com
Web: http://theartofservice.com | eLearning: http://theartofservice.org | Phone: +61 (0)7 3252 2055

## 2.1   *Implementation Plan/Project Plan*

# IT Services

## Implementation Plan/Project Plan

## Skeleton Outline

## Function: Service Desk

| Status: | In draft | |
| --- | --- | --- |
| | Under Review | |
| | Sent for Approval | |
| | Approved | |
| | Rejected | |
| Version: | <<your version>> | |
| Release Date: | | |

Copyright The Art of Service │ Brisbane, Australia │ Email: service@theartofservice.com
Web: http://theartofservice.com │ eLearning: http://theartofservice.org │ Phone: +61 (0)7 3252 2055

## Planning and implementation for Service Desk

*This document as described provides guidance for the planning and implementation for a Service Desk as described under the ITIL framework.*

*The document is not to be considered an extensive plan as its topics have to be generic enough to suit any reader for any organization.*

*However, the reader will certainly be reminded of the key topics that have to be considered for planning and implementation of this function.*

## Initial planning

When beginning the process planning the following items must be completed:

| CHECK ☺☺☹ or ✓× or date | DESCRIPTION |
|---|---|
| | Get agreement on the objective (use the ITIL definition), purpose, scope, and implementation approach (e.g. Internal, outsourced, hybrid) for the Service Desk. |

Copyright The Art of Service │ Brisbane, Australia │ Email: service@theartofservice.com
Web: http://theartofservice.com │ eLearning: http://theartofservice.org │ Phone: +61 (0)7 3252 2055

| | |
|---|---|
| | Assign a person to the key role of Service Desk manager/owner. This person is responsible for the Incident Management process and all associated systems.<br><br>However, it is important to understand the differences and common conflicts that can occur between the two roles, for example, the Service Desk Manager may be concerned with call volumes and answer times, whereas the Incident Manager may be concerned with percentage of resolution at first point of call. |
| | Conduct a review of activities that would currently be considered as an activity associated with this process. Make notes and discuss the "re-usability" of that activity.<br>Three key activities of the Service Desk are:<br><br>• Tracking, Monitoring and Coordinating of Incidents and Service Requests<br><br>• Incident Recording<br><br>• Incident Closure |
| | Create and gain agreement on a high-level associated process plans and a design for any associated process systems. NOTE: the plan need not be detailed. Too many initiatives get caught up in too much detail in the planning phase. **KEEP THE MOMENTUM GOING.** |

Copyright The Art of Service │Brisbane, Australia│ Email: service@theartofservice.com
Web: http://theartofservice.com │eLearning: http://theartofservice.org │Phone: +61 (0)7 3252 2055

| | Review the finances required for the Service Desk as a whole and any associated systems (expenditure including people, software, hardware, accommodation). Don't forget that the initial expenditure may be higher than the ongoing costs. Don't forget annual allowances for systems maintenance or customizations to systems by development staff. |
|---|---|

Copyright The Art of Service | Brisbane, Australia | Email: service@theartofservice.com
Web: http://theartofservice.com | eLearning: http://theartofservice.org | Phone: +61 (0)7 3252 2055

## Create Strategic statements

### Policy Statement

The policy establishes the "SENSE OF URGENCY" for the process.

It helps us to think clearly about and agree on the reasons WHY effort is put into this process.

An inability to answer this seemingly simple, but actually complex question is a major stepping stone towards successful implementation

The most common mistake made is that reasons regarding IT are given as the WHY we should do this. Reasons like *"to make our IT department more efficient"* are far too generic and don't focus on the real issue behind why this function is needed.

The statement must leave the reader in no doubt that the benefits of this function will be far reaching and contribute to the business in a clearly recognizable way.

### Objective Statement

When you are describing the end or ultimate goal for a unit of activity that is about to be undertaken you are outlining the OBJECTIVE for that unit of activity.

Of course the activity may be some actions for just you or a team of people. In either case, writing down the answer to WHERE will this activity lead me/us/the organization is a powerful exercise.

There are many studies that indicate the simple act of putting a statement about the

38

Copyright The Art of Service | Brisbane, Australia| Email:service@theartofservice.com
Web: http://theartofservice.com | eLearning: http://theartofservice.org | Phone: +61 (0)7 3252 2055

end result expected onto a piece of paper, then continually referring to it, makes achieving that end result realistic.

As a tip regarding the development of an objective statement; don't get caught up in spending hours on this. Do it quickly and go with your instincts or first thoughts – BUT THEN, wait a few days and review what you did for another short period of time and THEN commit to the outcome of the second review as your statement.

**Scope Statement**

In defining the scope of this process we are answering what activities and what "information interfaces" does this process have.

Don't get caught up in trying to be too detailed about the information flow into and out of this process. What is important is that others realize that information does in fact flow.

For example, with regard to the SERVICE DESK function we can create a simple table such as:

Copyright The Art of Service | Brisbane, Australia | Email: service@theartofservice.com
Web: http://theartofservice.com | eLearning: http://theartofservice.org | Phone: +61 (0)7 3252 2055

## Service Desk Information flows

| Process | | Process | Information |
|---|---|---|---|
| Service Desk | to | Problem Management | Incidents with unknown causes |
| Problem Management | to | Service Desk | Known Errors, Work-around, quick fixes |
| | | | |
| Service Desk | to | Change Management | Requests for Change |
| Change Management | to | Service Desk | Info on planned changes as the Service Desk may need to keep end users informed in the case of failed changes |
| | | | |
| Service Desk | to | Availability Management | Reports of availability-related incidents |
| Availability Management | to | Service Desk | Explanations regarding unacceptable levels of availability and solutions that the Service Desk can apply with end users. |

## Steps for Implementation

There can be a variety of ways to implement this function. For a lot of organizations a staged implementation may be suitable. For others a "big bang" implementation – due to absolute equality may be appropriate.

In reality however, we usually look at implementation according to pre-defined priorities. Consider the following **options**

40

Copyright The Art of Service │ Brisbane, Australia │ Email: service@theartofservice.com
Web: http://theartofservice.com │ eLearning: http://theartofservice.org │ Phone: +61 (0)7 3252 2055

and then apply a suitable model to your own organization or case study.

| STEPS | NOTES/ /RELEVANCE/DATES/WHO |
|---|---|
| Define the Objective and Scope for the Service Desk | |
| Establish and agree on a clear definition for the words "Incident", "Service / Support Request", "Problem", "Known Error" for the Service Desk staff.<br><br>This is one of the most interesting aspects. It can be very difficult to get everyone to agree to a definition, and it can be very difficult to establish the correct understanding of the definition.<br><br>However, get this right, and the rest of the Service Desk staff will find it easier to log tickets. | |
| Establish and Define Roles and Responsibilities for the process. Appoint a Service Desk Manager. | |

Copyright The Art of Service | Brisbane, Australia | Email: service@theartofservice.com
Web: http://theartofservice.com | eLearning: http://theartofservice.org | Phone: +61 (0)7 3252 2055

| | |
|---|---|
| Establish the physical environment for the Service Desk. <br><br> In running a 24 x 7 Service Desk it is important to be aware of local laws and customs with regards to minimum staffing levels during the night time shifts. | |
| Establish the Incident Management Process | |
| Tailor the ITSM Tools to suit the Incident Management process in line with the needs of the Service Desk. | |
| Establish and Define Relationship with all other processes. <br><br> This is another key aspect of the Service Desk. Service Desk will record all incidents that may pertain to any of the other processes. For example, Incidents resulting from Availability, Incidents resulting from Security, Incidents resulting from IT Service Continuity Management, Incidents resulting from Changes or Releases, etc. | |
| Establish monitoring levels. This will rely heavily on your telecommunications ability. Such things as integrated CTI technology will help. | |

Copyright The Art of Service | Brisbane, Australia | Email: service@theartofservice.com
Web: http://theartofservice.com | eLearning: http://theartofservice.org | Phone: +61 (0)7 3252 2055

| Define reporting standards | |
|---|---|
| Publicize and market | |

The priority selection has to be made with other factors in mind, such as competitive analysis, any legal requirements, and desires of "politically powerful influencers".

## Costs

The cost of process implementation is something that must be considered before, during and after the implementation initiative. The following points and table help to frame these considerations:

(A variety of symbols have been provided to help you indicate required expenditure, rising or falling expenditure, level of satisfaction regarding costs in a particular area, etc.)

| | Initial | During | Ongoing |
|---|---|---|---|
| **Personnel**<br><br>Costs of people for initial design of process, implementation and ongoing support | ✓ | 👇 | 👆 |
| **Accommodation**<br><br>Costs of housing new staff and any associated new equipment and space for documents or process related concepts. | 😐 | 🙂 | 🙁 |

Copyright The Art of Service | Brisbane, Australia | Email: service@theartofservice.com
Web: http://theartofservice.com | eLearning: http://theartofservice.org | Phone: +61 (0)7 3252 2055

| | | | |
|---|---|---|---|
| **Software**<br><br>New tools required to support the process and/or the costs of migration from an existing tool or system to the new one.<br><br>Maintenance costs | | | |
| **Hardware**<br><br>New hardware required to support the process activities. IT hardware and even new desks for staff. | | | |
| **Education**<br><br>Re-education of existing staff to learn new techniques and/or learn to operate new systems. | | | |
| **Procedures**<br><br>Development costs associated with filling in the detail of a process activity. The step-by-step recipe guides for all involved and even indirectly involved personnel. | | | |

In most cases, costs for Process / Function implementation have to be budgeted for (or allocated) well in advance of expenditure. Part of this step involves deciding on a charging mechanism (if any) for the new services to be offered.

## Build the team

Each process requires a process owner and in most situations a team of people to assist.

Copyright The Art of Service │ Brisbane, Australia│ Email: service@theartofservice.com
Web: http://theartofservice.com │ eLearning: http://theartofservice.org │ Phone: +61 (0)7 3252 2055

The Service Desk function is one of the Service Operation set that shows visible benefits from the outset and is very influential in setting the perception of IT Services to its customers and end users.

Of course a lot will be dependent on the timing of the implementation and whether it is to be staged or implemented as one exercise.

## Analyze current situation and FLAG

Naturally there are many organizations that have many existing procedures/processes and people in place that feel that the activities of the Service Desk is already being done. It is critical to identify these systems and consider their future role as part of the new process definition.

Examples of areas to review are:

| Area | Notes |
|---|---|
| Power teams | |
| Current formal procedures | |
| Current informal procedures | |
| Current role descriptions | |
| Existing organizational structure | |
| Spreadsheets, databases and other repositories | |
| Other… | |

Copyright The Art of Service │ Brisbane, Australia│ Email: service@theartofservice.com
Web: http://theartofservice.com │ eLearning: http://theartofservice.org │ Phone: +61 (0)7 3252 2055

## Implementation Planning

After base decisions regarding the scope of the Service Desk and the overall planning activities are complete we need to address the actual implementation of the function.

It is unlikely that there will not be some current activity or work being performed that would fit under the banner of this function. However, we can provide a comprehensive checklist of points that must be reviewed and done.

Implementation activities for Service Desk

| Activity | Notes/Comments/Time Frame/Who |
|---|---|
| Review current and existing Service Desk practices in greater detail. Make sure you also review current process connections from these practices to other areas of IT Service Delivery and Support. | |
| Review the ability of existing functions and staff. Can we "reuse" some of the skills to minimize training, education and time required for implementation? | |
| Establish the accuracy and relevance of current associated processes, procedures and meetings. As part of this step if any information is credible, document the transition from the current format to any new format that is selected. | |
| Decide how best to select any vendor that will provide assistance in this area (including tools, external consultancy or assistance to help with initial high workload during the implementation). | |

Copyright The Art of Service | Brisbane, Australia | Email: service@theartofservice.com
Web: http://theartofservice.com | eLearning: http://theartofservice.org | Phone: +61 (0)7 3252 2055

| | |
|---|---|
| Establish a selection guideline for the evaluation and selection of tools required to support this area (i.e. Service Desk tools). | |
| Purchase and install tools required to support this function (i.e. Service Desk tool). Ensure adequate skills transfer and on-going support is considered if external systems are selected. | |
| Create required business processes interfaces for this function that can be provided by the automated tools (e.g. reporting – frequency, content). | |
| Document and get agreement on roles, responsibilities and training plans. | |
| Communicate with and provide necessary education and training for staff that covers the actual importance of the function and the intricacies of being part of the Service Desk itself. | |

An important point to remember is that if the Service Desk is to be implemented at the same time as other processes then it is crucial that both implementation plans and importantly timing of work is complementary.

## Cutover to new function

The question of when a function actually starts is one that is not easy to answer. Most functional activity evolves without rigid starting dates and this is what we mean when we answer a question with "that's just the way it's done around here".

Ultimately we do want the new Service Desk to become the way things are done around here, so it may even be best not

Copyright The Art of Service | Brisbane, Australia | Email: service@theartofservice.com
Web: http://theartofservice.com | eLearning: http://theartofservice.org | Phone: +61 (0)7 3252 2055

to set specific launch dates, as this will set the expectation that from the given date all issues relating to the Service Desk will disappear (not a realistic expectation).

Copyright The Art of Service | Brisbane, Australia | Email: service@theartofservice.com
Web: http://theartofservice.com | eLearning: http://theartofservice.org | Phone: +61 (0)7 3252 2055

# IT Services

## Service Desk Technology Selection
## Function: Service Desk

| Status: | In draft | |
|---|---|---|
| | Under Review | |
| | Sent for Approval | |
| | Approved | |
| | Rejected | |
| Version: | <<your version>> | |
| Release Date: | | |

Copyright The Art of Service │ Brisbane, Australia │ Email: service@theartofservice.com
Web: http://theartofservice.com │ eLearning: http://theartofservice.org │ Phone: +61 (0)7 3252 2055

## Service Desk Technology Selection for Service Desk

*The document is not to be considered an extensive statement as its topics have to be generic enough to suit any reader for any organization.*

*However, the reader will certainly be reminded of the key topics that have to be considered.*

**This document serves as a reference for QUESTIONS THAT CAN HELP AN ORGANIZATION SELECT A TOOL for the Service Desk Function.**

**This document provides a basis for completion within your own organization.**

| This document was |
|---|
| Prepared by: _____ |
| On: <<date>> |
| And accepted by: _____ |
| On: <<date>> |

Copyright The Art of Service │ Brisbane, Australia│ Email: service@theartofservice.com
Web: http://theartofservice.com │ eLearning: http://theartofservice.org │ Phone: +61 (0)7 3252 2055

## Service Desk Technology Selection

The following is a list of questions that can be asked of key stakeholders and staff involved with the Service Desk and Service Management, to help define the requirements for a Service Desk.

The questions have been categorized into process segments.

The questions are designed to generate thought. Some of the questions may actually be more applicable during a scope and design phase and may not be asked during the exercise.

The purpose of this exercise is to gather the organization's requirements of what needs to be included in an IT Service Management tool. The requirements will be based on business needs and aligned to IT Service Management (ITSM) processes.

Collated answers can be used as an "ITSM Tool Requirements" document that can be used in future Request for Tenders (RFT). The document can also be provided to current tool vendors so that they may help the organization in changing their current tool environments to match the needs described in the ITSM Tool Requirements document.

It is important that when the organization implements ITSM processes that they have a supporting tool, to make those processes work as effectively as possible with minimal cost and disruption to the business.

The ITSM Tool Requirements document can list all the requirements discovered during the exercise. The document will not be a scope or design document detailing field requirements, naming of fields, technical effort or describe in any great detail each function within a tool.

Copyright The Art of Service | Brisbane, Australia | Email: service@theartofservice.com
Web: http://theartofservice.com | eLearning: http://theartofservice.org | Phone: +61 (0)7 3252 2055

# Processes

## Service Level Management

- Does the tool need to have the ability to add service levels?
- At what level are service levels to be added? i.e. Configuration Level, Contact Level, Organizational Level, Departmental Level, Locations level?
- How do you want control of the service levels managed?
- How do you want escalation of warnings to be carried out?
- In what medium do you need this carried out?
- How many levels of escalation do you need?
- Does escalation need to be sent to process owners?
- Does escalation need to be sent to IT Functional Managers?
- Does escalation need to be sent to IT Functional staff?
- Does escalation need to be sent to Business Managers?
- How do you see this happening?
- Do you need external escalation medium? (i.e. pager, mobile phone)
- How do you see the information contained in this area being needed or used in the areas listed below?
- Which report possibilities do you need?
- What sort of reports are you looking for?
- At what level do reports need to be created for?
- Do you need to be able to stop the clock ticking on SLAs?

## Incident Management

- Does the tool need to log incidents?
- How do you want incidents registered?
- Will the tool automatically detect incidents?
- What time stamping is needed?
- At what levels should categorization take place?

Copyright The Art of Service | Brisbane, Australia | Email: service@theartofservice.com
Web: http://theartofservice.com | eLearning: http://theartofservice.org | Phone: +61 (0)7 3252 2055

- Severity, Priority, Urgency or Impact, or all? – ITIL uses Urgency and Impact to determine Priority.
- Does the tool need to automatically allocate these priorities? Based on what requirements?
- What warnings are needed?
- What information needs to be stored on the incident ticket?
- How do you expect numbering to work?
- Is there a need to record Configuration Items?
- Is there a need to record linked Changes, Problems and other tickets to an incident?
- Will an incident automatically escalate?
- Will incidents be resolved then closed?
- When closing an incident what notifications need to be sent?
- Do notifications need to be sent?
- What information do you want to capture during the resolution of an incident?
- What information do you want to capture during the closing of an incident?
- What information do you want to capture during the investigation of the incident?
- Who will have access to the incident tickets? What information will they need?
- Do different users of the system need to see different information?
- Does the tool need to automatically prioritize multiple incidents?
- Do you want to capture the status of an incident? At how many levels? Will this need to change automatically?
- Do you need to add notes to the incident?
- Do you want users to be able to change the display?
- How do you see ownerships of tickets working?
- Does the tool need to be able to show related records based on contact, configuration item, categories, locations, etc?
- Do you want the tool to have the option for users to report an incident via mail?

Copyright The Art of Service | Brisbane, Australia | Email: service@theartofservice.com
Web: http://theartofservice.com | eLearning: http://theartofservice.org | Phone: +61 (0)7 3252 2055

- Are there any other methods to log an incident?
- Do you want to see SLA information on the incident ticket?
- What reports do you want for incident management?
- Do you want to record user input and user time stamps on the tickets? I.e. who did what and when and what they did or what they changed?
- Will a knowledge management database be linked to incident management?

**Problem Management**

- Does the tool need to support the ITIL process "Problem Management"?
- Does the tool need to register problem tickets as being separate from Incident tickets?
- Do you see this as another category?
- Does the tool need to register Known Errors?
- Do you see Known Errors as just another category on an incident ticket?
- Do you see problem tickets and known error tickets being logged manually and / or automatically?
- What time stamping do you need on the ticket?
- How do you want problem, and known error tickets categorized? Do they need to be categorized in the same manner as incident tickets?
- Do you want the following information captured?
  - Status of problem
  - Function responsible for the solution of the problem
  - Actions already taken
  - Problem solution
  - Work around

- Does the tool need to offer the option of dividing the total collection of problems into usable groups (e.g. equipment, network, data communications, work stations, etc.)?
- Do you want to capture the impact of the solution to parts of the IT-
  infrastructure or business?

Copyright The Art of Service | Brisbane, Australia | Email: service@theartofservice.com
Web: http://theartofservice.com | eLearning: http://theartofservice.org | Phone: +61 (0)7 3252 2055

- Do you need to capture Urgency, Impact and Priority on a problem ticket?

- What categorizations do you see on the ticket?

- Do you want escalations to occur from problem tickets?

- At what levels should escalations occur from problem tickets?

- Do escalations need to be sent to multiple people?

- Can escalations be sent to business people, i.e. contacts in the database?

- Will there be SLAs for problems?

- Do you need to record SLA data against problem tickets?

- What information do you need to capture on problem tickets?

Consider the following:

- Time spent for research and diagnosis per department or supplier?

- Short description of actions taken?

- Input of people needed?

- Input of resources needed?

- Costs?

- Descriptions of actions taken?

- Status?

- Service?

- Configuration Item?

- Time to solve a problem?

- Time expired for open problems?

- Expected time frames?

- Will the problem tickets show links to other tickets?

- Will a knowledge management database be linked to problem management?

Copyright The Art of Service | Brisbane, Australia | Email: service@theartofservice.com
Web: http://theartofservice.com | eLearning: http://theartofservice.org | Phone: +61 (0)7 3252 2055

## Service Asset & Configuration Management

- Does the management tool support the ITIL process of Configuration Management?

- Do you need the tool to have an integrated CMDB (Configuration Management Database)?

- How do you see the CMDB being populated?

- Who will maintain the CMDB? How do you see this working? What will the process be?

- Do you need the tool to be able to define a Configuration Item (CI), or will they be defined by a management tool?

- How do see the management tool defining a CI (e.g. hardware, software, network components, services etc.)?

- Do you want to capture relations between CIs? At what level? (This is where the strengths lie in Configuration Management tools and process)

- Do you need to see graphical representation of relationships?

- Do you need a status account for each CI? Do you want to record the lifecycle of the CI?

- At what level do you want to record CI?

- Do you need to record attributes of CIs? Do you have a list of key attributes?

- Will the management tool define the attributes or will a management tool do this?

- Do you want the tool to automatically create Asset IDs for CIs?

- Do you want to protect the CMDB from unauthorized use? Will only a select few people will have access to the CMDB?

- What levels of access will be needed to the CMDB?

- How do you see the CMDB relating to the other ITIL processes from a tool perspective?

- Do you expect to store associated documentation within the CMDB?

Copyright The Art of Service | Brisbane, Australia | Email: service@theartofservice.com
Web: http://theartofservice.com | eLearning: http://theartofservice.org | Phone: +61 (0)7 3252 2055

- Do you expect to manage licenses through the CMDB?
- Do you expect to record license information in the CMDB?
- Do you want the management tool to have the option to define and register a basic configuration and to save this separately (e.g. registration of the structure of (a part of) the IT infrastructure in a stable situation, so this can be consulted)?
- How do you see CIs being added or deleted?
- What naming conventions are needed? How will you determine the uniqueness of CIs?
- Does the tool allow unique identifiers?
- Do you need to capture model numbers, version numbers etc?
- What information do you see being captured against each CI?
- Should each CI form be different for each other CI? Will each CI form only show data that is needed for that CI? Will there be multiple CI forms?
- Is there an interface with the Incident, Change, Problem and Release tickets?
- Do you want cost information recorded? Do you want Maintenance information recorded?
- Will there be automatic alerts in the Configuration Management tool? What are the alerts that you want (e.g. changes, status changes, outages, maintenance schedules and tasks including responsibilities)?
- Will the CMDB be integrated into the tool?

## Change Management

- Does the management tool need to support ITIL processes?
- Does the management tool need a separate Change Management proposal?
- Does the management tool need to offer a standard change proposal that can be used by all employees within the organization?
- How do you want to classify Changes?
- Does the tool need to have a Forward Schedule of Changes? How do you see an FSC working within the tool?

Copyright The Art of Service | Brisbane, Australia | Email: service@theartofservice.com
Web: http://theartofservice.com | eLearning: http://theartofservice.org | Phone: +61 (0)7 3252 2055

- Do you need the tool to automatically save changes to the CMDB?
- Do you need to associate CIs to the RFC?
- Do you need to distinguish between different types of changes?
- Does the tool need to have different types of RFC forms for different changes?
- Does the tool need to have electronic signatures or a way for people to approve and disapprove changes?
- Some changes need multiple tasks carried out to achieve the change, how do you see this working in the management tool?
- Do you need the tool to register the causes of the change at such levels as, service levels, infrastructure, and organization?
- Do you expect to be able to record service levels against each RFC?
- What alerts do you see as needed in the tool?
- How do you see alerts being sent?
- What reports do you need to generate for Change Management?
- Does the business need to be involved in approving changes?
- What happens when a change is rejected?
- What happens when a change is accepted?
- What information do you need to record on a change?
- Does the tool need to link to any other modules or processes?
  Will reports be transparent to other applications (e.g. MS Office)?

## Release & Deployment Management

- Does the management tool need to support the process of Release Management?
- Does the management tool need to offer the option to indicate the status of a software product?
- What status indications do you need?
- Do you need a mechanism to control authorized and unauthorized status transitions?

58

- Does the management tool need to interface with a possible change management module? Why?
- Does it need to interface with a configuration management module? Why?
- How does the management tool structure the Definitive Software Library?
- How does the management tool structure the Definitive Hardware Store?
- Do you need the tool to have options regarding (total) overviews of software and breakdown facilities?
- Does the tool need to offer the option to perform semi-automatic fallback plans?
- Do you need to record the following information in the tool?
  - The number of licenses used
  - The users who use the applications
  - The version number of an application per user
  - The criticality of an application
  - The names of applications installed
  - The version number of all applications installed
  - License numbers of all applications installed
  - Number / amount of spending necessary for a fallback
  - Input of people and resources, specified by activity
  - Developments and expectations for the future
  - Deviations from the planning and budget

- How easy should it be to adapt or develop reports?
- Do reports need to be transparent to other applications?
- Which other links do you require from Release Management to other ITIL processes?

**Availability Management**
- Does the management tool need to support the ITIL processes?
- Should the tool offer an interface into the Service Level Management module?

Copyright The Art of Service | Brisbane, Australia | Email: service@theartofservice.com
Web: http://theartofservice.com | eLearning: http://theartofservice.org | Phone: +61 (0)7 3252 2055

- Should the management tool automatically generate a warning, should the agreed availability not be met?
- Do you need this warning to be sent to multiple process owners? Does it need to be sent to business management?
- How else do you see people being notified about a lack of availability?
- Does the management tool need to link to an incident or problem? Do you want the unavailability of (part of) the infrastructure to be linked to an event?
- Does the tool need to be proactive in determining possible availability levels in the future?
- Do you want to capture the following information?
    - Name of the system
    - Time period in which the measurements are performed
    - Total realized availability per defined system
    - Data and times on which the defined system was not available
    - Causes for the temporary unavailability of the defined system
    - Solutions for availability of the define system

- What reports do you want out of the tool?
- Which automatic links do you need in the tool?
- How will the tool integrate with other tools?
- Do you see this linking to the Configuration Management module?
- What information would you like to see passed between the modules?

Copyright The Art of Service | Brisbane, Australia | Email: service@theartofservice.com
Web: http://theartofservice.com | eLearning: http://theartofservice.org | Phone: +61 (0)7 3252 2055

## Capacity Management

- Does the management tool need to support the ITIL process?
- Does the management tool need to offer the option to generate the following information?
    - Name of the transaction processing system
    - Start and closing times
    - Total number of process transactions
    - Total period of time the CPU was in use
    - Total number of I/Os
    - Average memory capacity
    - Total paging rate
    - Total swapping rate
    - Breakdown of above mentioned information.

- Should the tool offer an interface into the Service Level Management module?
- Should the management tool automatically generate a warning, should the agreed capacity not be met?
- Do you need this warning to be sent to multiple process owners? Does it need to be sent to business management?
- How else do you see people being notified about a lack of capacity?
- Does the management tool need to link to an incident or problem? Do you want the capacity of (part of) the infrastructure to be linked to an event?
- Does the tool need to be proactive in determining possible capacity levels in the future?
- What reports do you want out of the tool?
- Which automatic links do you need in the tool?
- How will the tool integrate with other tools?
- Do you see this linking to the Configuration Management module?
- What information would you like to see passed between the modules?

Copyright The Art of Service | Brisbane, Australia | Email: service@theartofservice.com
Web: http://theartofservice.com | eLearning: http://theartofservice.org | Phone: +61 (0)7 3252 2055

## Financial Management

- Does the management tool need to support the ITIL process "Financial Management"?
- To what detail level do you want the structure of costs per SLA to be rendered?
- Where do you expect to see costs captured?
- Against which records in the tool do you see cost being captured?
- Do you see cost as being automatically calculated in the tool?
- Do you expect to capture charge rates for resources?
- Do you expect to associate charge rates for resources?
- What links do you see Financial Mgt having with other modules in the tool?
- Will there be penalties associated with breach of SLA and do you see the tool automatically capturing and calculating this?
- Do you expect to capture costs against Configuration Items?

## IT Service Continuity Management

- Does the management tool need to support the process of IT Service Continuity Management?
- How do you see a tool supporting the process of IT Service Continuity Management?
- Does the tool need to account or capture information regarding inadequate IT Continuity endangering the continuity of one or more business processes (not IT processes)?
- What links are needed from this process to the other ITIL processes?
- What other information do you see being captured?"

Copyright The Art of Service | Brisbane, Australia | Email: service@theartofservice.com
Web: http://theartofservice.com | eLearning: http://theartofservice.org | Phone: +61 (0)7 3252 2055

## Other Requirements

The tool vendor is to explain the functionality of the above processes as much as possible, in case the functionality are not handled by the above questions.

## General

- Do you expect that a knowledge management tool well be integral to the overall tool?
- At what level should there be search screens?
- Do users need the ability to tailor / change the output of the searches (e.g. can they add or remove extra columns of information)?
- Do you need users to be able to create their own searches?
- List all and any module you believe need to be in the tool.
- Do you want to be able to determine how tickets are numbered?
- What sort of flexibility in ticket numbering do you expect?
- Does the management tool need to offer the option of "job scheduling"?
- How do you see job scheduling notification working?
- Do you need to print from the management tool?

## Technical Requirements

- Should the tool be able to be integrated with Active Directory to enable single sign on?
- Should the tool come with its own proprietary database?
- Should the tool integrate with any specific databases?
- What other integration requirements are there?
- Who do you expect to tailor the tool?
- What level of technical complexity do you believe the tool should have?
- What level of IT expertise do you believe staff should have to tailor the tool?

Copyright The Art of Service | Brisbane, Australia | Email: service@theartofservice.com
Web: http://theartofservice.com | eLearning: http://theartofservice.org | Phone: +61 (0)7 3252 2055

## Requirements regarding support / maintenance

- What is your definition of support?
- What level of support do you require?
- Do you have time frames in mind for support?
- Do you want the support guaranteed via an SLA?

## Required Courses

- Are you going to send people on courses with regards to the tool?
- At what level do you require courses?
- How many people do you see going on courses?
- Are you going to rely on the vendor or the reseller to supply courses?
- What level of training do you people will need?

## Reports

- What reports do you believe need to come with the tool?
- Are you going to provide or do you have a third party reporting tool?
- What sort of reporting functionality do you require in the tool, if any?
- Do you want the vendor to supply you with a list of reports during a tender process?

## IT Information Security

- Does the tool need to offer the option of access control?
- What security requirements are needed in the tool?
- Does data need to be separated from functional groups?
- Does the organization have a naming and login convention or policy? Do you expect to be able to create your own naming conventions?
- Will anyone else external to the organization have access or need access to the tool and for what purposes?
- Do you want to be able to do the following?
  - Allocate users identification

64

- o Allocate (temporary) passwords
- o Define minimum password lengths
- o Command periodical changing of passwords
- o Register failed login attempts
- o Temporary close a workstation of (for example) three failed login attempts
- o Allocate users authorizations (access to certain parts of the IT infrastructure)
- o Allocate user rights within the authorized domains
- o Assure that previous allocated users identifications will not be re-allocated
- o Implement the single sign-on principle

**Reference Sites**

- How many reference sites do you want from the vendor?
- What are you looking for in a reference site?
- Do you want to see a site where the implementations weren't successful?
- Do you want to be able to visit the reference sites?
- How long would you like to spend at each reference site?

**Implementation**

- How much time during an implementation do you expect from the organization?
- How long do you expect an implementation to take?
- Do you want an estimate from a vendor?
- How do you see costs being shown by the vendor?
- How do you expect the vendor to show and describe the size of the implementation?

## 2.3 *Terminology*

65

Copyright The Art of Service | Brisbane, Australia | Email: service@theartofservice.com
Web: http://theartofservice.com | eLearning: http://theartofservice.org | Phone: +61 (0)7 3252 2055

**Incident Management:** To restore normal service operation as quickly as possible and minimize the adverse impact on business operations, thus ensuring that the best possible levels of service quality and availability are maintained.

**Problem Management:** To minimize the adverse impact of Incidents and Problems on the business that are caused by errors within the IT infrastructure, and to prevent the recurrence of Incidents related to these errors. Defined as two major processes: Reactive Problem Management, Proactive Problem Management **

**Service Asset & Configuration Management:** To support the agreed IT service provision by managing, storing and providing information about Configuration Items (CI's) and Service Assets throughout their life cycle. This process manages the service assets and Configuration Items in order to support the other Service Management processes.

**Change Management:** To ensure that standardized methods and procedures are used for efficient and prompt handling of all Changes, in order to minimize the impact of Change-related Incidents upon service quality, and consequently to improve the day-to-day operations of the organization.

**Release Management:** To deploy releases into production and establish effective use of the service in order to deliver value to the customer and be able to handover to Service Operation.

**Escalation:** This term is considered to replace notification. You can have two types of escalation, functional and / or hierarchical. Functional: to the people that will solve the problem, i.e. functional teams. Hierarchical: escalation to management, including managers of functional teams and managers of the business.

Copyright The Art of Service | Brisbane, Australia | Email: service@theartofservice.com
Web: http://theartofservice.com | eLearning: http://theartofservice.org | Phone: +61 (0)7 3252 2055

# IT Services

## Outsourcing Template

## Service Desk

| Status: | In draft | |
|---|---|---|
| | Under Review | |
| | Sent for Approval | |
| | Approved | |
| | Rejected | |
| Version: | <<your version>> | |
| Release Date: | | |

Copyright The Art of Service │ Brisbane, Australia │ Email: service@theartofservice.com
Web: http://theartofservice.com │ eLearning: http://theartofservice.org │ Phone: +61 (0)7 3252 2055

**Service Desk Outsourcing Template**

*The document is not to be considered an extensive statement as its topics have to be generic enough to suit any reader for any organization.*

*However, the reader will certainly be reminded of the key topics that have to be considered.*

**This document serves as a TEMPLATE FOR ENGAGING AN EXTERNAL PARTY TO MANAGE A SERVICE DESK. This document provides a basis for completion within your own organization.**

**This document contains prompts and text that would be meaningful for this activity.**

| | |
|---|---|
| This document was | |
| Prepared by: | _____ |
| On: | <<date>> |
| And accepted by: | _____ |
| On: | <<date>> |

Copyright The Art of Service │ Brisbane, Australia │ Email: service@theartofservice.com
Web: http://theartofservice.com │ eLearning: http://theartofservice.org │ Phone: +61 (0)7 3252 2055

# IT OUTSOURCING SERVICE AGREEMENT BETWEEN

_____

## AND

_____

THIS AGREEMENT between _____ ("OUTSOURCER") and _____ ("CLIENT") is made this ____ day of _____, ____.

WHEREAS, the CLIENT desires to purchase IT management and operation outsourcing services in support of the management and operation of the company's Information Technology need ; and

WHEREAS, OUTSOURCER wishes to provide the total outsourcing services described herein in accordance with the terms and conditions hereof;

NOW THEREFORE, in consideration of the payments herein agreed to be made and the covenants and agreement herein contained, the parties hereto, intending to be legally bound, hereby agree to the following:

## 1. SERVICES

Starting on the Effective Date (as defined in Section 3.1), OUTSOURCER shall perform the IT Outsourcing services described in this Agreement and Exhibit A, attached hereto and made a part hereof ("Scope of Services").

## 2. COST FOR SERVICES

The costs for services to be provided by OUTSOURCER are set forth in Exhibit B attached hereto and made a part hereof. Such costs shall be subject to a cost of living adjustment, as more fully set forth in Exhibit B.

Copyright The Art of Service | Brisbane, Australia | Email: service@theartofservice.com
Web: http://theartofservice.com | eLearning: http://theartofservice.org | Phone: +61 (0)7 3252 2055

## 3. TERMS AND CONDITIONS

### 3.1 Term:

This Agreement shall commence on _____, 19___ (the "Effective Date"), and terminate on _____, 19___.

### 3.2 Invoices and Payment Terms:

**3.2.1**   OUTSOURCER shall submit monthly invoices to the CLIENT. Invoices shall be issued before services are rendered by OUTSOURCER and shall be submitted by OUTSOURCER at least 30 business days before payment is due by the CLIENT.

**3.2.2**   Exhibit C indicates the monthly amounts to be paid by the CLIENT for OUTSOURCER staff services and expenses. The CLIENT shall pay according to this schedule. Payment not received within [five (5)] days of the due date will be subject to an interest charge. All interest charges will be computed at the current prime rate.

### 3.3 Data Processing Equipment and Supplies:

Subject to Section 3.9(c) below, as between the parties, the CLIENT reserves and retains the right, title and interest in any and all computing equipment, software, systems, data, output and other materials or property  except that which is furnished by OUTSOURCER **and is not developed pursuant to this Agreement,** which retains such rights itself. Upon expiration or earlier termination of this Agreement, OUTSOURCER shall relinquish to CLIENT the use of equipment provided by CLIENT in as good condition as when turned over to OUTSOURCER, reasonable wear and tear excepted.

Copyright The Art of Service │ Brisbane, Australia│ Email: service@theartofservice.com
Web: http://theartofservice.com │ eLearning: http://theartofservice.org │ Phone: +61 (0)7 3252 2055

**3.3.2** All costs relating to data processing equipment and supplies for the CLIENT's computer functions shall be the responsibility of the CLIENT.

**3.3.3** All costs relating to OUTSOURCER's consultants fee, salaries, Medical, Insurance, recruitment fee, training expenses shall be the responsibility of the OUTSOURCER.

**3.3.4** The CLIENT shall also provide to OUTSOURCER, at no charge to OUTSOURCER subject to Section 3.17 CLIENT Policy and Procedures, in order to allow OUTSOURCER to perform under this Agreement.

**(a)** All utilities, including any special power and air conditioning needed, **as determined solely by CLIENT**, to operate the CLIENT's data processing equipment and storage of computer supplies;

**(b)** Storage, in an area removed from the data processing site, for historical data and backup material that may be needed to reconstruct data files in the event working files are destroyed by natural disasters, fire, riots or other causes;

**(c)** Computing supplies such as paper, forms, ribbons, tapes, disk packs and microfilm; and

**(d)** Security, fire control equipment and janitorial support for the CLIENT's data processing facilities.

**3.4 Work Space:**

At no charge to OUTSOURCER, subject to Section 3.17 CLIENT Policy and

Copyright The Art of Service | Brisbane, Australia | Email: service@theartofservice.com
Web: http://theartofservice.com | eLearning: http://theartofservice.org | Phone: +61 (0)7 3252 2055

Procedures, the CLIENT shall provide OUTSOURCER, with an appropriately furnished, conveniently located office or other suitable work space for use by the OUTSOURCER staff in performing work under this Agreement. Also at no charge to OUTSOURCER, the CLIENT shall provide office supplies, telephone service and reproduction, telecommunications and office equipment reasonable and necessary to support OUTSOURCER's staff and performance of this Agreement.

**3.5 Use of Data Processing Equipment:**

At no charge to OUTSOURCER, subject to Section 3.17 CLIENT Policy and Procedures, the CLIENT shall provide OUTSOURCER access to all equipment, equipment services, programs and supplies necessary to support the computing needs of the CLIENT. The CLIENT shall provide OUTSOURCER's staffs access to all such equipment so that OUTSOURCER may perform its obligations under this Agreement including, but not limited to, operating all such equipment.

**3.6 Use of Software and Access to Personnel:**

For purposes of performance under this Agreement, OUTSOURCER shall have complete access to, shall operate and shall, subject to CLIENT's approval and obligations of CLIENT under third party agreements, have the right to modify or alter all CLIENT software programs and related material, pursuant to the Scope of Services. OUTSOURCER shall also have reasonable access to the CLIENT's management, professional and operating personnel necessary for performance under this Agreement, as well as to all materials, records, discs, tapes or other information necessary to perform the services contemplated herein. OUTSOURCER and CLIENT each realize that time are of the essence in order to accomplish the objectives of this Agreement, including the Scope of Services. OUTSOURCER agrees to respond to requests for support from CLIENT in a timely and reasonable manner. CLIENT agrees to handle OUTSOURCER's requests for support, to the best of its ability, in a timely

Copyright The Art of Service | Brisbane, Australia | Email: service@theartofservice.com
Web: http://theartofservice.com | eLearning: http://theartofservice.org | Phone: +61 (0)7 3252 2055

and reasonable manner.

## 3.7 Status Reporting:

OUTSOURCER management staff shall conduct regular meetings with the CLIENT **Contract** Administrator (as defined in Section 4.2.1 hereof) and such other persons as may be designated by the CLIENT to formally review OUTSOURCER performance under the terms of this Agreement. These meetings shall be conducted at a time and location mutually agreed upon.

OUTSOURCER shall also prepare, on a monthly and quarterly basis, as applicable, a written status report which documents past activities and outlines planned activities for the forthcoming month or year.

## 3.8 Non-Solicitation:

**3.8.1** Beginning on the Effective Date and continuing for a period of one year from the expiration or termination of this Agreement, the CLIENT shall not, without OUTSOURCER's prior written consent (which consent may be withheld at OUTSOURCER's sole discretion), enter into any **contract** (including, but not limited to, an employment **contract**, facilities management **contract** or consulting **contract**) with (i) any employee or former employee of OUTSOURCER who performed work under this Agreement within two years of such **contract** (an "OUTSOURCER Employee") or (ii) any person, firm, corporation or enterprise by which the OUTSOURCER Employee is employed or with which such OUTSOURCER Employee is affiliated (including, but not limited to, as a consultant, shareholder, partner, officer or director) ("OUTSOURCER Employee's New Firm"), whereby the OUTSOURCER Employee or OUTSOURCER Employee's New Firm would provide to the CLIENT all or part of the services provided by OUTSOURCER to the CLIENT under this Agreement.

Copyright The Art of Service | Brisbane, Australia | Email: service@theartofservice.com
Web: http://theartofservice.com | eLearning: http://theartofservice.org | Phone: +61 (0)7 3252 2055

**3.8.2** Beginning on the Effective Date and continuing for a period of one year from the expiration or termination of this Agreement, OUTSOURCER shall not, without CLIENT's prior written consent (which consent may be withheld at CLIENT's sole discretion), enter into any **contract** (including, but not limited to, an employment **contract**, facilities management **contract**, or consulting **contract**) with (i) CLIENT employee(s), or (ii) any person, firm, corporation or enterprise by which the CLIENT Employee is employed or with which such CLIENT Employee is affiliated (including, but not limited to, as a consultant, shareholder, partner, officer or director) ("CLIENT Employee's New Firm").

### 3.9 Confidentiality and Ownership of Material:

**3.9.1** Subject to paragraph (c) below, ownership of all data, material and documentation originated and prepared for the CLIENT pursuant to this Agreement shall belong exclusively to the CLIENT. Upon termination of the Agreement, all such data, material and documentation shall be returned by OUTSOURCER to the CLIENT.

**3.9.2** CLIENT and OUTSOURCER shall treat the other's "Confidential Information" (as defined below) as proprietary. Each of CLIENT an OUTSOURCER shall (i) exercise due care to keep in confidence and not disclose Confidential Information to any individual other than its own employees who have a "need to know" in order to perform the obligations of CLIENT or OUTSOURCER, as applicable, under this Agreement; (ii) not duplicate or publish any Confidential Information; and (iii) use Confidential Information only for the purposes authorized herein. The foregoing obligations shall not apply to Confidential Information if, and only to the extent that, it:

Copyright The Art of Service | Brisbane, Australia | Email: service@theartofservice.com
Web: http://theartofservice.com | eLearning: http://theartofservice.org | Phone: +61 (0)7 3252 2055

(a)   is or becomes public knowledge through no fault of either of the parties hereto

(b)   was previously known by the recipient;

(c)   is lawfully provided to the recipient without restriction by an independent third party; or

(d)   must be disclosed pursuant to applicable law or regulation; provided, however, that with respect to exception (a), the disclosing party (i.e., the party who is disclosing to a third party information which is confidential to the other party to this Agreement) shall first establish that the full particulars of the Confidential Information are, in the combination disclosed to the disclosing party, well known or generally used within the industry, not merely that the individual features are in the public domain or available in isolated segments in two or more readily-available public sources; and provided, further that the burden shall be on the disclosing party to prove the applicability of any of exceptions (a), (b), and (c).

**3.9.3**   For purposes hereof, "Confidential Information" shall mean manufacturing, engineering, software, business, customer, marketing, financial and other non-public information, reports or trade secrets relating to the business of OUTSOURCER or the CLIENT, as applicable, and created or learned by the CLIENT or OUTSOURCER, as applicable, in connection with the performance of this Agreement.

**3.9.4.1**   All worldwide right, title and interest in Intellectual Property Rights (as defined below) relating to in severable improvements in software and documentation not owned by or licensed to OUTSOURCER, which improvements are made,

Copyright The Art of Service | Brisbane, Australia | Email: service@theartofservice.com
Web: http://theartofservice.com | eLearning: http://theartofservice.org | Phone: +61 (0)7 3252 2055

conceived or developed by OUTSOURCER in the performance of its duties under this Agreement shall vest exclusively in CLIENT. In severable improvements shall mean those improvements that are not applicable to other software.

**3.9.4.2** All worldwide right, title and interest in Intellectual Property Rights in, to, or relating to new software, including without limitation, modules, subroutines and stand-alone programs, and related documentation made, conceived or developed by OUTSOURCER in the performance of its duties under this Agreement shall vest exclusively with CLIENT.

**3.9.4.3** All worldwide right, title and interest in Intellectual Property Rights in, to, or relating to severable improvements and modifications made, created, conceived or developed by OUTSOURCER in the performance of its duties under this Agreement, to software and related documentation not owned by or licensed to OUTSOURCER, shall vest exclusively in CLIENT. Severable improvements shall mean those improvements having application in and to other software.

**3.9.5** "Intellectual Property Rights" shall mean all patents, trade secrets, and copyrights in, covering, and relating to software and documentation made, created, conceived, developed, improved or modified by OUTSOURCER in the performance of its duties under this Agreement.

**3.9.6** Notwithstanding the foregoing to the contrary, Software developed under grants where OUTSOURCER is responsible for all aspects of development shall be done under a specific change of scope, and the ownership of the software so developed shall be governed by the grant provisions, and if there are no ownership requirements under the grant

Copyright The Art of Service | Brisbane, Australia | Email: service@theartofservice.com
Web: http://theartofservice.com | eLearning: http://theartofservice.org | Phone: +61 (0)7 3252 2055

provisions, then the provisions of subparagraph (d) shall apply.

**3.9.7** Notwithstanding the foregoing to the contrary, Software developed under grants where OUTSOURCER provides management and coordination services only shall not require a specific change of scope, and the ownership of the software so developed shall be governed by the grant provisions, and if there are no ownership requirements under the grant provisions, then the provisions of subparagraph 3.9.4 shall apply.

## 3.10 Liability and Warranties:

**3.10.1** **Subject to its record retention policies,** the CLIENT shall maintain Adequate Supporting Material to enable OUTSOURCER to update or regenerate, as necessary, data files, printer outputs and other data. In the event of loss, damage, destruction of any data, service, system or program due to the negligence of OUTSOURCER, OUTSOURCER's liability therefore shall be limited to either the replacement, repair, reconstruction, redevelopment or regeneration, at OUTSOURCER's option, of the lost, damaged, destroyed or inoperable data, service, system or program from the CLIENT's supporting material or otherwise as appropriate in the method deemed, most suitable, by OUTSOURCER for such action. In the event the CLIENT has failed to maintain Adequate Supporting Material, Outsourcer's liability shall be strictly limited to the same costs of replacement, repair, reconstruction, redevelopment or regeneration as if the CLIENT had so maintained adequate supporting material. Adequate Supporting Material is defined for the purposes of this Section as the original source material or data input documents initially provided to OUTSOURCER or replacement source material or data input documents provided to OUTSOURCER from time to time from which OUTSOURCER has obtained and input data in performance of its

Copyright The Art of Service | Brisbane, Australia | Email: service@theartofservice.com
Web: http://theartofservice.com | eLearning: http://theartofservice.org | Phone: +61 (0)7 3252 2055

services hereunder. OUTSOURCER shall not be liable for any damages resulting or arising from CLIENT's failure to perform its obligations hereunder, **provided that OUTSOURCER is not responsible for such failure to perform.**

3.10.2   **To the extent permitted Law**, OUTSOURCER shall not be liable, whether contractually or in tort, for any consequential, special or indirect damages arising out of or in connection with this Agreement. **To the extent they are beyond the reasonable control of OUTSOURCER**, OUTSOURCER shall not be responsible for schedule delays, inaccuracies or other consequences resulting from incorrect CLIENT data, lateness in delivery of CLIENT's data or the failure of CLIENT's equipment or personnel.

3.10.3   OUTSOURCER agrees to be liable for, defend and indemnify CLIENT against all claims, suits, judgments or damages, including the cost of administrative hearings, court costs and attorneys fees, arising out of the negligent or intentional acts or omissions, or violations of laws or regulations, of or on the part of OUTSOURCER or its agents, officers, subcontractors or employees, in the course of the operation of this Agreement.

3.10.4   **Warranties:** Outsourcer shall perform the services under this agreement in accordance with standards of care, skill and diligence consistent with recognized and prudent information technology practices, all applicable laws and regulations, the scope of services, exhibits, documents and procedures applicable to the services, and the degree of knowledge, skill and judgment normally exercised by professionals with respect to services of the same or similar nature. This is the only warranty made by outsourcer with respect to its services under this agreement and to the

Copyright The Art of Service | Brisbane, Australia | Email: service@theartofservice.com
Web: http://theartofservice.com | eLearning: http://theartofservice.org | Phone: +61 (0)7 3252 2055

extent permitted by laws is in lieu of all other understandings and all warranties, expressed, implied or statutory, as to the services to be provided by outsourcer, including but not limited to any warranty of merchantability or fitness for use for a particular purpose.

## 3.11 Taxes:

This Agreement does not include charges for any taxes, which now or in the future may be deemed by a taxing authority to be applicable to the services to be provided by OUTSOURCER. In the event a taxing authority determines now or in the future that such services are subject to tax,

OUTSOURCER shall invoice such taxes to the CLIENT and the CLIENT shall pay same simultaneously with the payment to which taxes relate.

CLIENT hereby represents that it is not currently subject to any such taxes and will notify OUTSOURCER in a timely manner if CLIENT becomes subject to any such tax. At the time of execution of this Agreement taxes on services provided by OUTSOURCER to CLIENT hereunder are not required to be paid, but if in the future are required, then CLIENT shall pay such taxes.

## 3.12 Force Majeure:

If either OUTSOURCER or the CLIENT is prevented from performing any task hereunder, in whole or in part, as a result of a cause beyond its reasonable control, which may include an Act of God, war, civil disturbance or **organized labor dispute,** such failure to perform shall not be grounds for termination of this Agreement.

## 3.13 Termination:

3.13.1    This Agreement may be terminated by a party (the "Terminating Party") prior to the expiration of its stated term upon the occurrence of an "Event

Copyright The Art of Service | Brisbane, Australia | Email: service@theartofservice.com
Web: http://theartofservice.com | eLearning: http://theartofservice.org | Phone: +61 (0)7 3252 2055

of Default" affecting the other party (the "Terminated Party")

**3.13.2**   An "Event of Default" shall mean:

**(a)**   failure by a party to timely perform any obligation under this Agreement, including without limitation CLIENT's failure to pay or cause to be paid any sums due in the manner provided in this Agreement within fifteen (15) business days of the date such payments were due; or OUTSOURCER not performing any of its obligations in accordance with this Agreement and all Exhibits thereto; or

**(b)**   any representation or warranty made by either party herein or in any document executed simultaneously and in connection herewith, or in any document or certificate furnished in connection herewith or therewith or pursuant hereto or thereto shall have been incorrect in any material respect at the time made; or

**(c)**   Upon the occurrence of an Event of Default the Terminating Party may give notice of termination to the Terminated Party, identifying in reasonable detail the nature of the Event of Default. Thereupon, the Terminated party shall have 30 days to correct in all material respects the Event of Default (15 business days if the Event of Default consists of CLIENT's failure to pay outstanding sums within 15 business days of the date the payment was due). If the Terminated party so cures the Event of Default, then the notice of termination shall be ineffective. If the Terminated party does not so cure the Event of Default within the aforementioned period, then this Agreement shall be

Copyright The Art of Service | Brisbane, Australia | Email: service@theartofservice.com
Web: http://theartofservice.com | eLearning: http://theartofservice.org | Phone: +61 (0)7 3252 2055

terminated upon the expiration of such period (the "Termination Date").

**3.13.3**   CLIENT shall pay OUTSOURCER in full, within 15 business days of receipt of a final invoice from OUTSOURCER, for all services rendered up to and including the Termination Date.

## 3.14 Phase Over:

**3.14.1**   Prior to the expiration pursuant to its term of this Agreement, OUTSOURCER shall develop a plan for the orderly transition of all services provided by OUTSOURCER under this Agreement (the "Transition Plan"). Such Transition Plan shall be developed by OUTSOURCER in conjunction with OUTSOURCER's employees on site, the CLIENT's executives and administrators and such other persons as shall be designated by the CLIENT. The CLIENT shall fully cooperate with OUTSOURCER in order to develop the Transition Plan. The Transition Plan shall be completed no later than 90 days prior to expiration of this Agreement. It shall cover, inter alia, the training of CLIENT's personnel in the operation and maintenance of the systems used and operated by OUTSOURCER during the term of the Agreement. CLIENT shall notify OUTSOURCER of its acceptance of the Transition Plan within 14 days of receipt from OUTSOURCER.

**3.14.2**   OUTSOURCER shall complete all transition activities associated with the orderly termination of this Agreement on or before the date the notice of termination becomes effective. OUTSOURCER shall effect the transition to the CLIENT.

**3.14.3**   If due to OUTSOURCER's actions or omissions (i) the Transition Plan is

Copyright The Art of Service | Brisbane, Australia | Email: service@theartofservice.com
Web: http://theartofservice.com | eLearning: http://theartofservice.org | Phone: +61 (0)7 3252 2055

not completed within the aforementioned period and the notice of termination becomes effective, or (ii) if the Transition Plan is completed and the notice of termination becomes effective but an orderly transition is not effected prior to the Termination Date, then OUTSOURCER shall continue to perform such services as may be required by the CLIENT, at no additional cost to CLIENT, in order to operate the CLIENT's computing system until such time as an orderly transition may be effected, but no later than 90 days after the Termination Date.

**3.14.4**   In the event of termination of this Agreement following the occurrence of an Event of Default on the part of OUTSOURCER, OUTSOURCER shall immediately upon the issuance of the notice of termination develop a Transition plan in accordance with the procedures set forth in paragraph (a) except, however, that the Transition Plan shall be completed no later than 30 days after the date of the notice of termination. CLIENT shall notify OUTSOURCER of its acceptance of the Transition Plan within 14 days of receipt from OUTSOURCER. OUTSOURCER shall complete all Transition activities associated with the termination by reason of its default no later than 60 days following OUTSOURCER's receipt of CLIENT's acceptance of the Transition Plan.

**3.14.5**   In the event of termination of this Agreement following the occurrence of an Event of Default on the part of CLIENT, then OUTSOURCER may, at the sole option of CLIENT, continue to perform such services as may be required by the CLIENT, at its rates then in effect, in order to operate the CLIENT's computing system until such time as an orderly transition may be effected, but no later than 90 days after the Termination Date; provided, however, that if the Event of Default consists in CLIENT's failure to pay any sums due OUTSOURCER, then OUTSOURCER shall continue to perform such services as may be required by the CLIENT

Copyright The Art of Service | Brisbane, Australia | Email:service@theartofservice.com
Web: http://theartofservice.com | eLearning: http://theartofservice.org | Phone: +61 (0)7 3252 2055

after the Termination Date, at OUTSOURCER's rates then in effect, only if the CLIENT pays for such services in advance.

## 3.15 Funding:

**3.15.1**   CLIENT hereby represents to OUTSOURCER that (i) the services to be performed by OUTSOURCER hereunder are necessary to CLIENT's efficient operation of its business and (ii) to the best of its knowledge, after investigation, it believes that sufficient funds may be obtained by it or appropriated for it in order to make all payments contemplated hereby.

**3.15.2**   CLIENT shall make its best efforts to obtain, or cause to be appropriated as part of CLIENT's annual budget, sufficient funds to pay the sums due from time to time hereunder.

## 3.16 Independent Contractor Status:

OUTSOURCER and CLIENT acknowledge and agree that OUTSOURCER is and shall be an independent
contractor; that neither OUTSOURCER nor any of its employees, representatives or agents is, or shall be deemed to be, an employee, partner or joint venture of the CLIENT; and that neither OUTSOURCER nor any of its employees, representatives or agents shall be entitled to any employee benefits under any employee benefit plan, including medical, insurance and other similar plans, of the CLIENT. OUTSOURCER further acknowledges that the CLIENT will not withhold any amounts in respect to local taxes
from amounts payable by the CLIENT hereunder and it shall be the exclusive responsibility of OUTSOURCER to pay all amounts due in respect of applicable federal, state and local taxes on such amounts.

Copyright The Art of Service | Brisbane, Australia | Email: service@theartofservice.com
Web: http://theartofservice.com | eLearning: http://theartofservice.org | Phone: +61 (0)7 3252 2055

### 3.17 Client Policy and Procedures:

OUTSOURCER agrees to comply with all applicable CLIENT policies and procedures, including but not limited to those regarding conditions of work, access to and use of CLIENT's offices, facilities, work space, support services, supplies, Data Processing Equipment and software and access.

## 4. MISCELLANEOUS PROVISIONS

### 4.1 Severability:

Each provision of this Agreement shall be a separate and distinct covenant and, if declared illegal, unenforceable or in conflict with any governing law, shall not affect the validity of the remaining portion of this Agreement.

### 4.2.1 Client's Contract Administrator:

The CLIENT shall appoint as **Contract** Administrator

_____, who will be delegated the duty and responsibility of maintaining liaison with OUTSOURCER and to oversee performance of this Agreement.

### 4.2.2 OUTSOURCER's Contract Administrator:

The Outsourcer shall appoint as **Contract** Administrator

_____, who will be delegated the duty and responsibility of maintaining liaison with CLIENT and to oversee performance of this Agreement.

### 4.3 Successors:

This Agreement and all future amendments shall be binding on parties and their heirs,

Copyright The Art of Service | Brisbane, Australia | Email: service@theartofservice.com
Web: http://theartofservice.com | eLearning: http://theartofservice.org | Phone: +61 (0)7 3252 2055

successors and assigns. The CLIENT agrees that OUTSOURCER may pledge or assign the net sums of money due and to become due to it hereunder to any bank, lending agency or institution as collateral security.

## 4.4 Renewal/Extension:

Upon written agreement of both parties entered into at least ninety (90) days prior to the expiration date, this Agreement may be extended for successive one year periods on the terms and conditions then in effect subject however, to such modifications as may be set forth in the extension agreement.

## 4.5 Entire Agreement-Amendments:

**(a)** This Agreement, together with the Exhibits hereto, embodies the entire agreement and understanding between the parties hereto and supersedes all prior understandings and agreements, whether written or oral, between the parties hereto relating to the matter hereof.

**(b)** This Agreement (including the Exhibits hereto) may not be amended or modified except in writing signed by the parties hereto.

## 4.6 Assignment

This Agreement may not be assigned by either party without the prior written consent of the other party. **For the avoidance of doubt, a change of control of OUTSOURCER shall not constitute an assignment for purposes hereof.**

## 4.7 Attorneys Fees

Copyright The Art of Service | Brisbane, Australia | Email: service@theartofservice.com
Web: http://theartofservice.com | eLearning: http://theartofservice.org | Phone: +61 (0)7 3252 2055

In the event that suit is brought to enforce the provisions of this Agreement, the prevailing party, as determined by the judge, or arbitrator in the event of arbitration, shall be entitled to an award of reasonable attorneys' fees, paralegals' fees and court costs, whether incurred before trial, at trial, during appeals, or in any mediation or arbitration required by a court.

Copyright The Art of Service | Brisbane, Australia | Email: service@theartofservice.com
Web: http://theartofservice.com | eLearning: http://theartofservice.org | Phone: +61 (0)7 3252 2055

## 2.5  Service Desk Metrics

Metrics should be established so that performance of the Service Desk can be evaluated at regular intervals. This is important to assess the health, maturity, efficiency, effectiveness and any opportunities to improve Service Desk operations.

Metrics for Service Desk performance must be realistic and carefully chosen. It is common to select those metrics that are easily available and that may seem to be a possible indication of performance; however, this can be misleading. For example, the total number of calls received by the Service Desk is not in itself an indication of either good or bad performance and may in fact by caused by events completely outside the control of the Service Desk – for example a particularly busy period for the organization, or the release of a new version of a major corporate system.

An increase in the number of calls to the Service Desk can indicate less reliable services over that period of time – but may also indicate increased user confidence in a Service Desk that is maturing, resulting in a higher likelihood that users will seek assistance rather than try to cope alone. For this type of metric to be reliable for reaching either conclusion, further comparison of previous periods for any Service Desk improvements implemented since the last measurement baseline, or service reliability changes, problems, etc. to isolate the true cause for the increase is needed.

Further analysis and more detailed metrics are therefore needed and must be examined over a period of time. These will include the call-handling statistics, and additionally:

- The first-line resolution rate: the percentage of calls resolved at first line, without the need for escalation to support other groups. This is the figure often

Copyright The Art of Service | Brisbane, Australia | Email: service@theartofservice.com
Web: http://theartofservice.com | eLearning: http://theartofservice.org | Phone: +61 (0)7 3252 2055

quoted by organizations as the primary measure of the Service Desks performance – and used for comparison purposes with the performance of other desks – but care is needed when making any

comparisons. For greater accuracy and more valid comparisons this can be broken down further as follows:

- The percentage of calls resolved during the first contact with the Service Desk, i.e. while the user is still on the telephone to report the call

- The percentage of calls resolved by the Service Desk staff themselves without having to seek deeper support from other groups. Note: some desks will choose to co-locate or embed more technically skilled second-line staff with the Service Desk. In such cases it is important when making comparisons to also separate out (i) the percentage resolved by the Service Desk staff alone; and (ii) the percentage resolved by the first-line Service Desk staff and second-line support staff combined.

- Average time to resolve an incident (when resolved at first line)

- Average time to escalate an incident (where first-line resolution is not possible)

- Average Service Desk cost of handling an incident. Two metrics should be considered here:

- Total cost of the Service Desk divided by the number of calls. This will provide an average figure which is useful as an index and for planning purposes but does not accurately represent the relative costs of different types of calls

- By calculating the percentage of call duration time on the desk overall and

Copyright The Art of Service | Brisbane, Australia | Email: service@theartofservice.com
Web: http://theartofservice.com | eLearning: http://theartofservice.org | Phone: +61 (0)7 3252 2055

working out a cost per minute (total costs for the period divided by total call duration minutes) this can be used to calculate the cost for individual calls and give a more accurate figure.

- By evaluating the types of incidents with call duration, a more refined picture of cost per call by types arises and gives an indication of which incident types tend to cost more to resolve and possible targets for improvements.

- Percentage of customer or user updates conducted within target times, as defined in SLA targets

- Average time to review and close a resolved call

The number of calls broken down by time of day and day or week, combined with the average call-time metric, is critical in determining the number of staff required.

Copyright The Art of Service | Brisbane, Australia | Email: service@theartofservice.com
Web: http://theartofservice.com | eLearning: http://theartofservice.org | Phone: +61 (0)7 3252 2055

## 2.6 Communication Plan

# IT Services

## Communication Plan

## Function: Service Desk

| Status: | In draft | |
| --- | --- | --- |
| | Under Review | |
| | Sent for Approval | |
| | Approved | |
| | Rejected | |
| Version: | <<your version>> | |
| Release Date: | | |

Copyright The Art of Service | Brisbane, Australia | Email: service@theartofservice.com
Web: http://theartofservice.com | eLearning: http://theartofservice.org | Phone: +61 (0)7 3252 2055

# Communication Plan for the Service Desk

*The document is not to be considered an extensive statement as its topics have to be generic enough to suit any reader for any organization.*

*However, the reader will certainly be reminded of the key topics that have to be considered.*

This document serves as a GUIDE FOR COMMUNICATIONS REQUIRED for the Service Desk function. This document provides a basis for completion within your own organization.

This document contains suggestions regarding information to share with others. The document is deliberately concise and broken into communication modules. This will allow the reader to pick and choose information for e-mails, flyers, etc. from one or more modules if and when appropriate.

| This document was | |
|---|---|
| Prepared by: | _____ |
| On: | <<date>> |
| And accepted by: | _____ |
| On: | <<date>> |

Copyright The Art of Service | Brisbane, Australia | Email: service@theartofservice.com
Web: http://theartofservice.com | eLearning: http://theartofservice.org | Phone: +61 (0)7 3252 2055

## Initial Communication

### Sell the Benefits

First steps in communication require the need to answer the question that most people (quite rightly) ask when the IT department suggests a new system, a new way of working. WHY?

It is here that we need to promote and sell the benefits. However, be cautious of using generic words. Cite specific examples from your own organization that the reader will be able to relate to (to help develop specific examples contact service@theartofservice.com for competitive quotation).

| Generic Benefit statements | Specific Organizational example |
|---|---|
| Service Desk provides a single point of contact for our customers and end-users | This is important because… |
| Allows us to manage all incidents and the registration of RFCs and Service requests. | Our last Customer Satisfaction Survey shows that our customers are not satisfied with the way we handle their calls for help… |
| Helps us to more effectively manage our communications to the business. | Apart from the obvious benefits of communication, the specific reason why we bring this up is… |
| The Service Desk will assist the other process areas with some operational activities…. | IT staff are more and more buried under administration type activities and this is affecting the quality of their work. Wouldn't it be wonderful if…. |

Copyright The Art of Service | Brisbane, Australia | Email: service@theartofservice.com
Web: http://theartofservice.com | eLearning: http://theartofservice.org | Phone: +61 (0)7 3252 2055

# Service Desk Goal

## The Goal of the Service Desk

---

**The Goal of the Service Desk can be promoted in the following manner.**

<u>Official Goal Statement</u>: **To support the agreed IT service provision by ensuring the accessibility and availability of the IT-organization and by performing various supporting activities.**

- High visibility and wide channels of communication are essential in this function. Gather specific Service Desk Requirements from nominated personnel

(Special Tip: Beware of using only Managers to gain information from, as the resistance factor will be high)

- Oversee the registration and resolution of incidents to ensure that the business needs of IT are not impacted more than necessary.
- Provide relevant reports to nominated personnel.

(Special Tip: Beware of reporting only to Managers. If you speak to a lot of people regarding Service Delivery then you need to establish ways to report to these people the outcomes and progress of the discussions).

Always bear in mind the "so what" factor when discussing areas like goals and objectives. If you cannot honestly and sensibly answer the question "so what" – then you are not selling the message in a way that is personal to the listener and gets their "buy-in".

---

Copyright The Art of Service | Brisbane, Australia | Email: service@theartofservice.com
Web: http://theartofservice.com | eLearning: http://theartofservice.org | Phone: +61 (0)7 3252 2055

| The above Communication module was distributed |
| To: _____ |
| On: &lt;&lt;date&gt;&gt; |
| |
| By: _____ |
| On: &lt;&lt;date&gt;&gt; |

## Service Desk Activities

Copyright The Art of Service | Brisbane, Australia | Email: service@theartofservice.com
Web: http://theartofservice.com | eLearning: http://theartofservice.org | Phone: +61 (0)7 3252 2055

The list of actions in this module may have a direct im

curious as to why all of a sudden they have to call the

Blogs in IT, like they used to do. There could be an el

different strategies to overcome this initial skepticism.

**Call logging (activity for Incident Mgt.)**

- Set out clear procedures to submit incidents
- Set out clear procedures when incidents are

**Verify CMDB (activity for Conf. Mgt)**

- As part of the registration, classification and
  Service Desk staff will ask specific questions

**Monitor progress**

- All incidents that come in to the Service Des
  through the various processes (incident Mar
  Management, Change Management). The n
  Service Desk is also the first point of contac
  customers and end-users.

**End-user training**

- In some organizations it is the Service Desk
  induction training, desktop training and othe

**Pro-Active activities**

- As the Service Desk staff talk to the custome
  the week, they should be able to point out to
  the areas for improvement are.

**Customer Satisfaction Surveys**

- One of the communications to the customer
  satisfaction survey. The Service Desk staff c
  out to the customers (or ask the questions o
  responses and publish the results.

Copyright The Art of Service | Brisbane, Australia | Email: service@theartofservice.com
Web: http://theartofservice.com | eLearning: http://the

**Communication to customers**

- Service Desk staff send out reports, notificat
  and end-users to:

Copyright The Art of Service | Brisbane, Australia | Email: service@theartofservice.com
Web: http://theartofservice.com | eLearning: http://theartofservice.org | Phone: +61 (0)7 3252 2055

# Service Desk Planning

## Costs

Information relating to costs may be a topic that would be held back from general communication. Failure to convince people of the benefits will mean total rejection of associate costs. If required, costs fall under several categories:

- Personnel – Service Desk staff

- Accommodation – Physical location (Set-up and ongoing)

- Software – Tools (Set-up and ongoing)

- Hardware – Infrastructure (Set-up)

- Education – Training (Set-up and ongoing)

- Procedures – external consultants etc (Set-up)

The costs of implementing a Service Desk will be outweighed by the benefits. For example, many organizations have a negative perception of their IT department because of inaccessibility of the key people.

A well run Service Desk will make major inroads into altering that perception.

---

Details regarding the cost of Service Desk were distributed

To: _____

On: <<date>>

By: _____

On: <<date>>

Copyright The Art of Service | Brisbane, Australia | Email: service@theartofservice.com
Web: http://theartofservice.com | eLearning: http://theartofservice.org | Phone: +61 (0)7 3252 2055

## 2.7 *Business Flyers*

# IT Services

## Service Desk

## Business and IT Flyers

| Status: | In draft | |
| --- | --- | --- |
| | Under Review | |
| | Sent for Approval | |
| | Approved | |
| | Rejected | |
| Version: | <<your version>> | |
| Release Date: | | |

Copyright The Art of Service │ Brisbane, Australia│ Email: service@theartofservice.com
Web: http://theartofservice.com │ eLearning: http://theartofservice.org │ Phone: +61 (0)7 3252 2055

## Introduction

The following pages provide 3 examples of flyers that can printed and distributed throughout your organization.

They are designed to be displayed in staff rooms.

Note, they are examples, and your input is required to complete the flyers.

Remember, the important thing is to ensure that the message delivered in the flyer is appropriate to the audience that will be reading it.

So think about how and where you will be distributing the flyers.

Copyright The Art of Service | Brisbane, Australia | Email: service@theartofservice.com
Web: http://theartofservice.com | eLearning: http://theartofservice.org | Phone: +61 (0)7 3252 2055

# IT Service Desk

## IT Services Department

## Wanted: Improved IT Services

**Key Points:**

- Faster Response Times.

- Quicker Resolution.

- Services You Need.

- Services at the Right Time!

- Improved IT Services

- Less Disruption

- << any additional points >>

The IT Department is constantly improving on the services we deliver. Our most recent focus has been on the Service Desk.

<< Provide brief description of the roles and responsibilities of the Service Desk >>

First, determine the audience of this flyer. This could be anyone who might benefit from the information it contains, for example, IT employees or Business staff.

Where are you going to send this flyer? Which locations will the flyer be posted at?

If you are posting the flyer in staff rooms, then the content needs to reflect the information that will be of use to them. For example, list the benefits to them for calling the Service Desk instead of trying to call $2^{nd}$ and $3^{rd}$ Line Support directly. This will help set the expectations.

What process do they need to follow when recording information about failures in IT Services? What information should they have ready?

Provide phone numbers for the Service Desk.

| BENEFITS | PROCESS | CONTACTS |
|---|---|---|
| List the benefits to the intended audience | List the steps involved in the process | List the contacts |
| Keep it simple | Keep it simple | Input any graphics in here |
| Use bullet points | Show steps as necessary and beneficial | |

Copyright The Art of Service | Brisbane, Australia | Email: service@theartofservice.com
Web: http://theartofservice.com | eLearning: http://theartofservice.org | Phone: +61 (0)7 3252 2055

Copyright The Art of Service | Brisbane, Austra
Web: http://theartofservice.com | eLearning: http://th

Your report has to be with the CEO in one hour.
**BUT YOUR PC ISN'T WORKING!**

The Service Desk is here to help. The Service Desk provides 1$^{st}$ line support for all IT issues. By logging a ticket we can track your issue until it is resolved, keeping you in the loop the whole time.

## IT SERVICE DESK

Copyright The Art of Service | Brisbane, Australia | Email: service@theartofservice.com
Web: http://theartofservice.com | eLearning: http://theartofservice.org | Phone: +61 (0)7 3252 2055

## 2.8 ITIL V3 Incident Management Process Flow Diagram

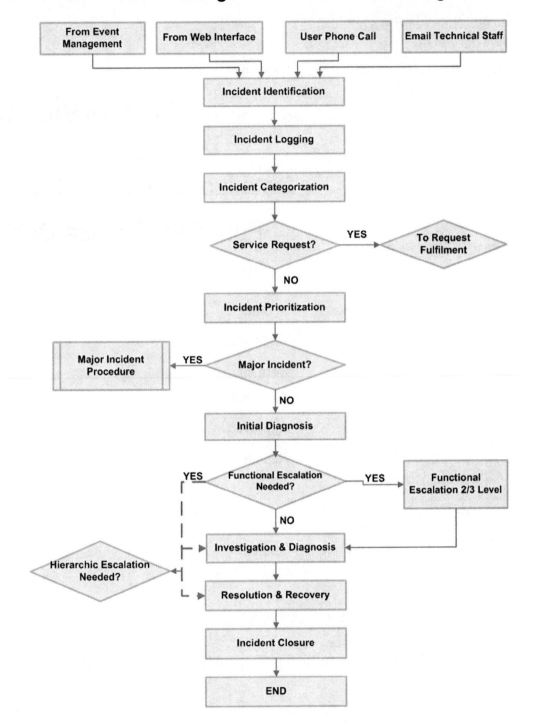

Copyright The Art of Service │ Brisbane, Australia│ Email: service@theartofservice.com
Web: http://theartofservice.com │ eLearning: http://theartofservice.org │ Phone: +61 (0)7 3252 2055

# IT Services

## Detailed Objectives/Goals

## Function: Service Desk

| Status: | In draft | |
| --- | --- | --- |
| | Under Review | |
| | Sent for Approval | |
| | Approved | |
| | Rejected | |
| Version: | <<your version>> | |
| Release Date: | | |

Copyright The Art of Service | Brisbane, Australia | Email: service@theartofservice.com
Web: http://theartofservice.com | eLearning: http://theartofservice.org | Phone: +61 (0)7 3252 2055

## Detailed Objectives/Goals for Service Desk

*The document is not to be considered an extensive statement as its topics have to be generic enough to suit any reader for any organization.*

*However, the reader will certainly be reminded of the key topics that have to be considered.*

**The detailed objectives for Service Desk should include the following salient points:**

| Objective | Notes |
|---|---|
| **Improve Customer Satisfaction**<br><br>By providing a single point of contact for the customers and end-users you will make the accessibility of the IT department higher. This will improve customer satisfaction as they now know where to go to when they have a question or IT issue.<br><br>Don't forget to include the IT staff as end-users in the survey. One of the main improvements should be that the Service Desk takes a lot of workload off the IT specialists. | Met/Exceeded/Shortfall<br><br>☺ ☺ ☹<br><br>Dates/names/role titles |

Copyright The Art of Service | Brisbane, Australia| Email: service@theartofservice.com
Web: http://theartofservice.com | eLearning: http://theartofservice.org | Phone: +61 (0)7 3252 2055

| | |
|---|---|
| **Responsiveness**<br><br>When a customer / end-user contacts the Service Desk they should be looked after swiftly.<br><br>By monitoring the responsiveness of the SD staff you can improve the perception that the customer / end-user has of the IT department.<br><br>Accessibility of the IT department is one of the main objectives of a Service Desk. It shouldn't be difficult to get in touch with the Service Desk.<br><br>(You probably don't speak highly of a Service Desk where you have to wait 2 minutes on the phone before somebody picks up) | |
| Establish **efficient reporting lines**<br><br>Service Desk staff also play a major part in the communication from the IT department back to the customers / end-users.<br><br>IT should be clear who reports on what and why.<br><br>SD staff very often send out the monthly performance reports to the customers on behalf of the SLM process. | |

Copyright The Art of Service | Brisbane, Australia | Email: service@theartofservice.com
Web: http://theartofservice.com | eLearning: http://theartofservice.org | Phone: +61 (0)7 3252 2055

| | |
|---|---|
| **Professional image** of the IT department<br><br>With a well established Service Desk and experienced, pro-active, friendly staff the image of the IT department will be more positive.<br><br>The Service Desk should focus on a professional work ethic and approach. | |
| **To establish ground rules that distinguish a genuine request for Incident as opposed to a Service Request.**<br>*Request for information* or *status of a service* (not related to loss of service) *Includes Standard Changes.* E.g. Contact details, Service availability, request for common software.<br><br>. There will however, be a detailed procedure about when and how passwords are to be reset and who is to be advised, etc. – but approval from the Incident Manager is not required. | |

Copyright The Art of Service │ Brisbane, Australia │ Email: service@theartofservice.com
Web: http://theartofservice.com │ eLearning: http://theartofservice.org │ Phone: +61 (0)7 3252 2055

| | |
|---|---|
| **Develop working relationships with all other process areas**.<br><br>The Service Desk is a pivotal one with regard to requiring input from other process areas. Obvious links include Incident Management (SD staff are first point of call for incidents and record all incidents that come in), Configuration Management (to verify configuration information) and Release Management (sending out release notices). Less obvious links include Financial Management for IT Services (to establish Return on Investment (ROI) on incidents and the cost per call) and IT Service Continuity Management (to the level of Service Desk support during a contingency situation). | |
| **Develop a SD that suits the organization and look for continuous improvement.**<br><br>A Service Desk can be designed in various ways: you can have a local service Desk, or a distributed Service Desk. Some organizations even opt for a virtual Service Desk to make it easier to support the 'follow the sun' concept.<br><br>What type of Service Desk suits your organization? How does this SD design support the overall Service Desk goals and business goals? | |

Use these objectives to generate discussion about others that may be more appropriate to list than those provided.

Copyright The Art of Service │ Brisbane, Australia│ Email: service@theartofservice.com
Web: http://theartofservice.com │ eLearning: http://theartofservice.org │ Phone: +61 (0)7 3252 2055

# IT Services

## Policies, Objectives and Scope
## Function: Service Desk

| Status: | In draft | |
| --- | --- | --- |
| | Under Review | |
| | Sent for Approval | |
| | Approved | |
| | Rejected | |
| Version: | <<your version>> | |
| Release Date: | | |

Copyright The Art of Service | Brisbane, Australia | Email: service@theartofservice.com
Web: http://theartofservice.com | eLearning: http://theartofservice.org | Phone: +61 (0)7 3252 2055

# Policies, Objectives and Scope for Service Desk

*This document is not to be considered an extensive statement as its topics have to be generic enough to suit any reader for any organization.*

*However, the reader will certainly be reminded of the key topics that have to be considered.*

## Policy Statement

**A course of action, guiding principle, or procedure considered expedient, prudent, or advantageous**

Use this text box to answer the "SENSE OF URGENCY" question regarding this function.

Why is effort being put into this function?
Not simply because someone thinks it's a good idea. That won't do. The reason has to be based in business benefits.

You must be able to concisely document the reason behind starting or improving this function.

Is it because of legal requirements or competitive advantage? Perhaps the business has suffered major problems or user satisfaction ratings are at the point where outsourcing is being considered.

A policy statement any bigger than this text box, may be too lengthy to read, lose the intended audience with detail, not be clearly focused on answering the WHY question for this process.

Copyright The Art of Service | Brisbane, Australia | Email: service@theartofservice.com
Web: http://theartofservice.com | eLearning: http://theartofservice.org | Phone: +61 (0)7 3252 2055

The above Policy Statement was

Prepared by: _____

On: &lt;&lt;date&gt;&gt;

And accepted by: _____

On: &lt;&lt;date&gt;&gt;

Copyright The Art of Service │ Brisbane, Australia │ Email: service@theartofservice.com
Web: http://theartofservice.com │ eLearning: http://theartofservice.org │ Phone: +61 (0)7 3252 2055

## Objectives Statement

Something worked toward or aimed for; a goal.

Copyright The Art of Service | Brisbane, Australia | Email: service@theartofservice.com
Web: http://theartofservice.com | eLearning: http://theartofservice.org | Phone: +61 (0)7 3252 2055

Use this text box to answer the "WHERE ARE W

this function.

**Generic sample Mission statement for Service De**

Service Desk Mission Statement: The Service Desk a

service provision by ensuring the accessibility and av

and by performing various supporting activities.

- To provide a helpful and friendly first point of c
- To provide basic support for computing and au
- To provide the necessary online forms to requ
  network account changes.
- To provide online FAQ's, manuals, and tutoria
  troubleshoot.
- To provide equipment delivery and repair serv

What will be the end result of this function and how wi

reached the end result?

Will we know because we will establish a few key met

a more subjective decision, based on instinct?

**A generic sample statement on the "objective" for**

**The Service Desk function provides a single point**

**of the IT department, not only for incidents and qu**

**activities such as Change requests and SLM repo**

**desk represents the IT department to the custome**

**such is key in the customer satisfaction and perce**

Copyright The Art of Service | Brisbane, Australia | Email: service@theartofservice.com
Web: http://theartofservice.com | eLearning: http://theartofservice.org | Phone: +61 (0)7 3252 2055

Note the keywords in the statement. **For the stateme**

**"representative, customer satisfaction, perceptior**

The above Objective Statement was

Prepared by: _____

On: <<date>>

And accepted by: _____

On: <<date>>

Copyright The Art of Service | Brisbane, Australia | Email: service@theartofservice.com
Web: http://theartofservice.com | eLearning: http://theartofservice.org | Phone: +61 (0)7 3252 2055

## Scope Statement

The area covered by a given activity or subject

Use this text box to answer the "WHAT" question regarding this function.

What are the boundaries for this function?
What does the information flow look like into this function and from this function to other processes?

**A generic sample statement on the "scope" for Service Desk is:**

**The Service Desk function will be responsible for managing first line support and general customer contact involving all aspects of the IT Service Operation. The Service Desk will be responsible for the daily verification of the CMDB.**

**Service Desk will not be responsible for problem analysis and management of changes.**

A scope statement any bigger than this text box, may be too lengthy to read, lose the intended audience with detail, not be clearly focused on answering the WHAT question for this process.

Be aware that the scope of the Service Desk depends on the way the IT department is organized. It can be as broad or narrow as needed. You might wish to use Service Desk staff to perform simple activities for the other processes, i.e. performing routine changes, updating databases, sending out reports.

Copyright The Art of Service │Brisbane, Australia│ Email: service@theartofservice.com
Web: http://theartofservice.com │ eLearning: http://theartofservice.org │ Phone: +61 (0)7 3252 2055

## 2.11 *Business justification document*

# IT Services

## Business Justification

## Function: Service Desk

| Status: | In draft | |
| --- | --- | --- |
| | Under Review | |
| | Sent for Approval | |
| | Approved | |
| | Rejected | |
| Version: | <<your version>> | |
| Release Date: | | |

Copyright The Art of Service │ Brisbane, Australia│ Email: service@theartofservice.com
Web: http://theartofservice.com │ eLearning: http://theartofservice.org │ Phone: +61 (0)7 3252 2055

# Business Justification Document for Service Desk

*The document is not to be considered an extensive statement as its topics have to be generic enough to suit any reader for any organization.*

*However, the reader will certainly be reminded of the key topics that have to be considered.*

**This document serves as a reference for HOW TO APPROACH THE TASK OF SEEKING FUNDS for the implementation of the Service Desk Function.**

**This document provides a basis for completion within your own organization.**

| | |
|---|---|
| This document was | |
| Prepared by: | _____ |
| On: | \<\<date>> |
| And accepted by: | _____ |
| On: | \<\<date>> |

Copyright The Art of Service | Brisbane, Australia | Email: service@theartofservice.com
Web: http://theartofservice.com | eLearning: http://theartofservice.org | Phone: +61 (0)7 3252 2055

## Service Desk Business Justification

A strong enough business case will ensure progress and funds are made available for any IT initiative.

This may sound like a bold statement but it is true. As IT professionals we have (for too long) assumed that we miss out on funds while other functional areas (e.g. Human resources and other shared services) seem to get all that they want.

However, the problem is not with them, it's with US. We are typically poor salespeople when it comes to putting our case forward.

We try to impress with technical descriptions, rather than talking in a language that a business person understands.

For example:

| We say | We should say |
|---|---|
| We have to increase IT security controls, with the implementation of a new firewall. | Two weeks ago our biggest competitor lost information that is now rumored to be available on the internet. |
| The network bandwidth is our biggest bottleneck and we have to go to a switched local environment. | The e-mail you send to the other national managers will take 4 to 6 hours to be delivered. It used to be 2 to 3 minutes, but we are now using our computers for many more tasks. |
| Changes to the environment are scheduled for a period of time of minimal business impact. | We are making the changes on Sunday afternoon. There will be less people working then. |

Copyright The Art of Service | Brisbane, Australia | Email: service@theartofservice.com
Web: http://theartofservice.com | eLearning: http://theartofservice.org | Phone: +61 (0)7 3252 2055

Doesn't that sound familiar?

To help reinforce this point even further, consider the situation of buying a new fridge. What if the technically savvy sales person wants to explain "the intricacies of the tubing structure used to super cool the high pressure gases, which flow in an anti-clockwise direction in the Southern hemisphere".

Wouldn't you say "too much information, who cares – does it make things cold?"

Well IT managers need to stop trying to tell business managers about the tubing structure and just tell them what they are interested in.

So let's know look at some benefits of Service Desk. Remember that the comments here are generic, as they have to apply to any organization. If you need assistance in writing business benefits for your organization please e-mail service@theartofservice.com for a quotation.

| Benefits | Notes/Comments/Relevance |
|---|---|
| Introduces a structured support system, where each person has a common and concise view on the function of the Service Desk in the organization. | |

Copyright The Art of Service │Brisbane, Australia│ Email: service@theartofservice.com
Web: http://theartofservice.com │eLearning: http://theartofservice.org │Phone: +61 (0)7 3252 2055

| | |
|---|---|
| Reduces the reliance on key staff to perform multiple duties.<br><br>Depending on the model of Service Desk support there can be a shift from subject matter experts spending a high degree of time working on administrative tasks, to actually helping people.<br><br>The properly managed Service Desk will also have built in redundancy with respect to the people involved, so that there is always back-up and resources available should one person be absent. | |
| With the co-introduction of a sound Incident Management and Problem Management processes the Service Desk will move away from a function that is continually in a "fire-fighting" mode to one that delivers true value-added support to the organization. | |

Copyright The Art of Service │ Brisbane, Australia │ Email: service@theartofservice.com
Web: http://theartofservice.com │ eLearning: http://theartofservice.org │ Phone: +61 (0)7 3252 2055

| | |
|---|---|
| A professional Service Desk will quickly start to change any negative perception that customers or end-users will have.<br><br>This change cannot be expected simply by launching the Service Desk. The communication plan that announces the new service must also be carefully planned and implemented. | |
| The new Service Desk structure will bring to an end (or else significantly reduce) the number of unrecorded requests for assistance and unauthorized changes to the IT infrastructure.<br><br>While people are involved with the function there will always be "by-passing", however, the checks and reporting structures for this function will help to reduce this. | |

Copyright The Art of Service | Brisbane, Australia | Email: service@theartofservice.com
Web: http://theartofservice.com | eLearning: http://theartofservice.org | Phone: +61 (0)7 3252 2055

| | |
|---|---|
| A new Service Desk function is often accompanied with a new Service Desk tool.<br><br>This combined with a standard education base for all staff helps the same problems being resolved repeatedly rather than eliminated<br><br>Such steps lead to immediate results in not having to solve the same problem multiple times, as staff learn how to search for any occurrence of the problem as well as how to record incidents to allow for easier faster searching. | |
| The reporting structure that will be designed with the new function allows more meaningful information to be delivered.<br><br>Such reporting has more of a business focus, rather than a traditional focus on reporting the number of calls received or resolved at first point of contact.<br><br>With this new business focus managers are much more empowered to justify the costs of running their areas of responsibility, as they can know demonstrate real business returns. | |

Copyright The Art of Service | Brisbane, Australia | Email: service@theartofservice.com
Web: http://theartofservice.com | eLearning: http://theartofservice.org | Phone: +61 (0)7 3252 2055

# IT Service Management (ITSM) Capability Assessment

## Based on ITIL® Version 3

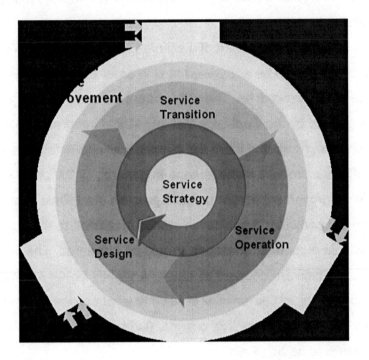

## *Service Operation Questionnaire*

Copyright The Art of Service | Brisbane, Australia | Email: service@theartofservice.com
Web: http://theartofservice.com | eLearning: http://theartofservice.org | Phone: +61 (0)7 3252 2055

# 3 Introduction

This document is one part of a broader assessment model enabling you to establish the extent to which your organization has adopted the good practice guidance for IT Service Management (ITSM) based on the Information Technology Infrastructure Library (ITIL) version 3.

The assessment scheme is composed of a simple questionnaire which enables you to ascertain which areas should be addressed next in order to improve the overall quality and performance of ITIL processes. The assessment is based on the generic capability levels defined by the Capability Maturity Model Integrated (CMMI) framework, which recognizes that there are a number of characteristics which need to be in place for effective process management. In general, CMMI provides guidance for efficient, effective improvement across multiple process disciplines in an organization.

To establish where a particular organization stands in relation to the process capability framework, a variable number of questions should be answered. The questions are weighted, i.e. those which are deemed as having a slightly higher significance are considered mandatory for a 'Yes' answer at each level of capability. These questions are denoted by a 'M' symbol in the 'No' column, (indicating that a 'Yes' answer is required if the level is to be achieved).

The assessment is used to establish a baseline of current practices in the organization and to assist in the development of improvement initiatives for processes that can be used when they:

- Decide what services they should be providing, define standard services, and let people know about them
- Make sure they have everything they need to deliver a service, including people, processes, consumables, and equipment
- Get new systems in place, change existing systems, retire obsolete systems, all while making sure disruption to existing services and customers is minimized
- Set up agreements, take care of service requests, and operate services

Copyright The Art of Service | Brisbane, Australia | Email: service@theartofservice.com
Web: http://theartofservice.com | eLearning: http://theartofservice.org | Phone: +61 (0)7 3252 2055

- Make sure they have the resources needed to deliver services and that services are available when needed—at an appropriate cost
- Handle what goes wrong—and prevent it from going wrong in the first place if possible
- Ensure they are ready to recover from potential disasters and get back to delivering services if the disaster occurs

Although it is conceptually feasible to improve all processes, it is not economical to improve all processes to level 5. Therefore the results of the capability assessment should be analyzed in conjunction with the defined business objectives and stakeholders' priorities for improvement.

Copyright The Art of Service | Brisbane, Australia | Email: service@theartofservice.com
Web: http://theartofservice.com | eLearning: http://theartofservice.org | Phone: +61 (0)7 3252 2055

Scoring model for assessing process capability

There are five levels defined within the CMMI framework, as predictability, effectiveness and control of an organization's processes are believed to improve as the organization moves up these five levels.

| Capability Level | General characteristics |
|---|---|
| Level 0 – Non-existent | Investigation shows no existing process goals and an effective lacking of process activities being employed. |
| Level 1 – Performed (Ad-hoc) | Processes at this level are typically undocumented and in a state of dynamic change, tending to be driven in an ad hoc, uncontrolled and reactive manner by users or events. This provides a chaotic or unstable environment for the processes.<br><br>In general, the process supports and enables the work needed to provide<br>Services, but improvements may be lost over time. |

Copyright The Art of Service | Brisbane, Australia | Email: service@theartofservice.com
Web: http://theartofservice.com | eLearning: http://theartofservice.org | Phone: +61 (0)7 3252 2055

| Level 2 - Managed | A managed process is a performed (capability level 1) process that has the basic infrastructure in place to support the process. It is planned and executed in accordance with policy; employs skilled people who have adequate resources to produce controlled outputs; involves relevant stakeholders; is monitored, controlled, and reviewed; and is evaluated for adherence to its process description. The process discipline reflected by capability level 2 helps to ensure that existing practices are retained during times of stress. |
| | There may be a high reliance on individual skill level due to inconsistent documentation or training made available. |

Copyright The Art of Service | Brisbane, Australia | Email: service@theartofservice.com
Web: http://theartofservice.com | eLearning: http://theartofservice.org | Phone: +61 (0)7 3252 2055

| Level 3 – Defined | A defined process is a managed (capability level 2) process that is tailored to be effective under various environmental conditions and with a range of appropriate inputs.<br><br>At capability level 3, the standards, process descriptions, and<br>procedures for a project are tailored from the organization's set of<br>standard processes to suit a particular project or organizational unit and<br>therefore are more consistent, except for the differences allowed by the tailoring guidelines.<br><br>At capability level 3, processes are managed more proactively using an understanding of the interrelationships of the process activities and detailed measures of the process and its work products. |
|---|---|
| Level 4 - Quantitatively Managed | A quantitatively managed process is a defined (capability level 3) process that is controlled using statistical and other quantitative techniques. Quantitative objectives for quality and process performance are established and used as criteria in managing the process. Quality and process performance is understood in statistical terms and is managed throughout the life of the process. |

Copyright The Art of Service | Brisbane, Australia | Email: service@theartofservice.com
Web: http://theartofservice.com | eLearning: http://theartofservice.org | Phone: +61 (0)7 3252 2055

| Level 5 – Optimizing | An optimizing process is a quantitatively managed (capability level 4) process that is improved based on an understanding of the common causes of variation inherent in the process. The focus of an optimizing process is on continually improving the range of process performance through both incremental and innovative improvements. |
|---|---|

Copyright The Art of Service | Brisbane, Australia | Email: service@theartofservice.com
Web: http://theartofservice.com | eLearning: http://theartofservice.org | Phone: +61 (0)7 3252 2055

Directions for conducting assessment

Follow these steps to ascertain the organizational capability level for a specific ITSM process:

- Start at Level 1 and answer each question, ticking 'Y' or 'N' column as appropriate;
- Check the level criteria given at the foot of the table of Level 1 questions. If the criteria for Level 1 are satisfied, move on to the next level;
- Continue up the levels until the criteria for the current level are not entirely met. For example, should the criteria be satisfied for Levels 1, 2, 3, but are not quite met for Level 4, then no further questions need be attempted and the organization's capability level is deemed to be 3.

Copyright The Art of Service | Brisbane, Australia | Email: service@theartofservice.com
Web: http://theartofservice.com | eLearning: http://theartofservice.org | Phone: +61 (0)7 3252 2055

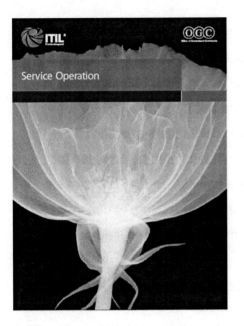

The Service Operation lifecycle phase is primarily focused on the management of IT Services that ensures effectiveness and efficiency in delivery and support. Successful Service Operation requires coordination and execution of the activities and processes required to deliver and manage services at agreed levels to business users and customers. Service Operation is also responsible for ongoing management of the technology that is used to deliver and support services.

One of Service Operation's key roles is dealing with the conflict between maintaining the status quo, adapting to the changing business and technological environments and achieving a balance between conflicting sets of priorities.

As the centre point for the majority of activity in an IT organization, Service Operation will be faced with many challenges in achieving a balance between all varying objectives defined and perspectives that are required. Perspectives that are considered include:

- Technology – focusing on ensuring a consistent architecture, the effective functioning of individual components and continually investigating and leveraging new technologies being developed
- IT Service Management – focusing on executing and performing the processes that optimize the cost and quality of service delivered
- Organization – focusing on the capabilities being provided that enable the business to meet its objectives, enhanced productivity for users and support for future business growth.

Copyright The Art of Service | Brisbane, Australia | Email: service@theartofservice.com
Web: http://theartofservice.com | eLearning: http://theartofservice.org | Phone: +61 (0)7 3252 2055

# 4  Event Management

The goal of Event Management is to provide the capability to detect events, make sense of them and determine the appropriate control action. Event Management is therefore the basis for Operational Monitoring and Control.

Event Management should be utilized to detect and communicate operational information as well as warnings and exceptions, so that input can be provided for reporting the service achievements and quality levels provided. It may be used for automating routine activities such as backups and batch processing, or dynamic roles for balancing demand for services across multiple infrastructure items/sources to improve performance.

- Event Management can be applied to any aspect of Service Management that needs to be controlled and which can be automated. These include:
- CIs - to provide visibility of functioning and failing components, or to understand when other changes have occurred in the infrastructure
- Environmental conditions – such as increases in the temperature of servers and facilities
- Software license monitoring – used to maintain optimum licensing utilization
- Security – to perform security checks and to detect exceptions or intrusions
- Normal activity – such as tracking the activity and performance of an IT service.

It is important to note the difference between monitoring and Event Management. While the two areas are related, Event Management focuses on the generation and detection of notifications about the status of the IT infrastructure and services. Monitoring on the other hand has a broader scope, which will include monitoring CIs that do not generate events or alerts. So when implementing Event Management, consideration should be made as to what monitoring activities and techniques should be interfaced to generate alerts and notifications that will provide value to the IT groups and wider organization.

Copyright The Art of Service | Brisbane, Australia | Email: service@theartofservice.com
Web: http://theartofservice.com | eLearning: http://theartofservice.org | Phone: +61 (0)7 3252 2055

| Level 1 – Performed (Ad-hoc) | Y | N |
|---|---|---|
| There is some level of event monitoring and alert generation occurring across the organization. | | M |
| Mechanisms are in place to detect service affecting events, so that an incident can be logged and appropriate correction action taken. | | M |
| There are some thresholds in place to identify potential disruptions (e.g. caused by slow performance, 10% remaining capacity on storage device etc.) and warn the appropriate group/individual. | | |
| Measures have been taken to filter events so that neither too many or too little alerts are being generated. | | |
| Events that show normal operation (information events) are captured where necessary. | | |
| **Minimum score to achieve this level:**     **'Y' for all mandatory ('M') questions** <br><br>                        **+**   **1 other 'Y'** <br><br> **answer** | | |

| Level 2 – Managed | Y | N |
|---|---|---|
| There is a formal policy and guidelines defined for Event Management to be used in the organization. | | M |
| Critical systems and devices are monitored to detect events occurring. | | M |

Copyright The Art of Service | Brisbane, Australia | Email: service@theartofservice.com
Web: http://theartofservice.com | eLearning: http://theartofservice.org | Phone: +61 (0)7 3252 2055

| | | |
|---|---|---|
| Training or awareness sessions have been conducted or made available electronically for staff, providing guidelines and instructions for how to employ the Event Management process. | | M |
| The definition of an Event is clearly understood and distinguished from an incident, problem or service request. | | M |
| There are guidelines defined for a number of roles and responsibilities associated with Event Management. | | M |
| Information and guidelines for event monitoring, thresholds and corrective actions are provided by the service/system designers and architects. | | |
| There are systems that provide capabilities for logging and storing events, and generating alerts. | | |
| There are documented guidelines for when and how an incident should be logged as a result of exception events. | | |
| Event data is used by design processes (e.g. Capacity and Availability Management) when formulating the design of a service or service change. | | |
| **Minimum score to achieve this level:** **'Y' for all mandatory ('M') questions** **+ 2 other 'Y' answers** | | |

Copyright The Art of Service | Brisbane, Australia | Email: service@theartofservice.com
Web: http://theartofservice.com | eLearning: http://theartofservice.org | Phone: +61 (0)7 3252 2055

| Level 3 – Defined | Y | N |
|---|---|---|
| Each infrastructure or application team have documented the Event Management systems being used by their team. | | M |
| SLAs are used to design safeguards for services, ensuring that wherever possible, warnings are generated to notify of a potential breach. | | M |
| A number of auto-response workflows have been implemented, allowing automated actions and checks to be performed without human intervention. | | M |
| A range of communication systems are used for the transmission of alerts, including: email, SMS and the built-in messaging features of the ITSM tool(s). | | M |
| Clear roles and responsibilities have been identified, defined, documented and appointed for the Event Management process. | | M |
| The Configuration Management System is used to relate current and historical events with Configuration Items. | | |
| Ownership is assigned and maintained for any escalated events. | | |
| An operational team completes a regular health check of the IT infrastructure at least weekly, checking event records as part of the assessment. | | |
| Event Management provides data to Release & Deployment during the distribution and early life of a release. | | |
| The Information Security Management policy defines what security and access events must be recorded, and what follow-up actions are required. | | |

Copyright The Art of Service | Brisbane, Australia | Email: service@theartofservice.com
Web: http://theartofservice.com | eLearning: http://theartofservice.org | Phone: +61 (0)7 3252 2055

| | Y | N |
|---|---|---|
| Event Management provides data to Capacity Management and Availability Management for both design and operational activities. | | |
| Where the response to an event requires a standard change, there is a document procedure describing the steps to be taken. | | |
| **Minimum score to achieve this level:**     **'Y' for all mandatory ('M') questions** <br><br>                              **+   3 other 'Y'** <br><br> **answers** | | |

| Level 4 – Quantitatively Managed | Y | N |
|---|---|---|
| Relative standards and other quality criteria applicable for the registration of events and any follow-up actions are made clear to the Event Management team. | | M |
| The organization will set and review targets or objectives for Event Management on a regular basis. | | M |
| Regular reviews are held to determine shortfalls or weak areas of Event Management, using Incident and Problem data to guide improvement actions. | | M |
| Incidents are tracked to ensure that resolution timeframes documented in SLAs are met, with any potential breaches being flagged and escalated to the appropriate party for resolution. | | |
| Reports are regularly produced that shows how Event Management is contributing to the reduction in number and impact of service disruptions. | | |

Copyright The Art of Service │ Brisbane, Australia │ Email: service@theartofservice.com
Web: http://theartofservice.com │ eLearning: http://theartofservice.org │ Phone: +61 (0)7 3252 2055

| | Y | N |
|---|---|---|
| The process owner will sample random event records to determine process compliance. | | |
| Trends in the workload of Event Management is reported on and utilized to identify the staffing requirements for various work periods. | | |
| Actions are taken to identify and reduce the number of 'false alerts' being generated. | | |
| **Minimum score to achieve this level:** **'Y' for all mandatory ('M') questions** <br><br> **+ 2 other 'Y'** <br><br> **answers** | | |

| Level 5 – Optimizing | Y | N |
|---|---|---|
| The cost and value of Event Management is quantified: this is used to assist in calculating and validating the Total Cost of Ownership (TCO) of services. | | M |
| There is a mechanism for staff to document areas of weakness for Event Management, such as devices or components without event detection capabilities. Regular reviews seek to take corrective action if justified. | | M |
| Event Management provides data related to Service Validation & Testing in order to better support future test designs and test models. | | |
| Event Management provides data for process and service improvement initiatives. | | |
| Incident Management provides Incident reference information to Event Management for Event/Incident cross reference. This seeks to enhance the early detection and resolution of exceptions. | | |

Copyright The Art of Service | Brisbane, Australia | Email: service@theartofservice.com
Web: http://theartofservice.com | eLearning: http://theartofservice.org | Phone: +61 (0)7 3252 2055

| Minimum score to achieve this level:    'Y' for all mandatory ('M') questions<br><br>                                       +   1 other 'Y'<br><br>answer | |
| --- | --- |

Copyright The Art of Service │ Brisbane, Australia │ Email: service@theartofservice.com
Web: http://theartofservice.com │ eLearning: http://theartofservice.org │ Phone: +61 (0)7 3252 2055

# Incident Management

The goal of Incident Management is to restore normal service operation as quickly as possible and minimize the adverse impact on business operations, thus ensuring that the best possible levels of service quality and availability are maintained. Normal service operation is defined as operating within the agreed Service Level Agreement (SLA) limits.

Incident Management can be utilized to manage any event which disrupts, or has the potential to disrupt an IT service and associated business processes. Careful distinction needs to be made between the role of Event Management and Incident Management, as only events that indicate exception to normal service operation and are determined by the Event Correlation engine to be significant are escalated to Incident Management. This means that incident records may be generated as a result of:

- End users calling the Service Desk to notify of a disruption to their normal use of IT services
- Events representing an exception that are resolved using automated means, with an associated incident record also being generated for informational purposes
- An IT staff member noticing that a component of the IT infrastructure is behaving abnormally, despite no current impact on the end user community
- An end user logging an incident using self help means, which is then resolved by IT operations staff
- An external supplier observes that a portion of the IT infrastructure under their control is experiencing issues, and logs a incident ticket via email.

While the process of Request Fulfillment does typically operate in a similar fashion to Incident Management, a service request does not involve any (potential) disruption to an IT service.

Copyright The Art of Service | Brisbane, Australia | Email: service@theartofservice.com
Web: http://theartofservice.com | eLearning: http://theartofservice.org | Phone: +61 (0)7 3252 2055

| Level 1 – Performed (Ad-hoc) | Y | N |
|---|---|---|
| Incident records are logged and maintained for all reported incidents. | | M |
| Incident Management exists as a consistent and repeatable process across our organization. | | M |
| There is a defined method for calculating incident priority that is based on the relative business impact and urgency of the disruption. | | |
| Incident Management provides the Service Desk or Customer/User with progress updates on the status of incidents (or the user can view the incident record via self-help). | | |
| Incident Management uses consistent methods to confirm closure of the incident. | | |
| **Minimum score to achieve this level:** **'Y' for all mandatory ('M') questions** **+ 1 other 'Y'** **answer** | | |

| Level 2 – Managed | Y | N |
|---|---|---|
| There is a procedure or system for classifying incidents, with a detailed set of categorization and prioritization codes. | | M |
| An incident database or ticketing system is maintained to record details for all reported incidents. | | M |
| Training or awareness sessions have been conducted or made available electronically for staff, providing guidelines and instructions for how to employ the Incident Management process. | | M |

Copyright The Art of Service | Brisbane, Australia | Email: service@theartofservice.com
Web: http://theartofservice.com | eLearning: http://theartofservice.org | Phone: +61 (0)7 3252 2055

| | | |
|---|---|---|
| The definition of a Major Incident based on impact and urgency is clearly understood. A procedure for handling a Major Incident is defined, documented and followed. | | **M** |
| There are guidelines defined for a number of roles and responsibilities associated with Incident Management. | | **M** |
| Response and resolution times for incidents are defined in accordance with agreed targets documented in Service Level Agreements (SLAs). | | |
| Incident managers are empowered to enforce agreed customer service levels with second line support and third party suppliers. | | |
| An Incident Management process owner with accountability for the process across the organization has been appointed. | | |
| A policy exists that documents rules for escalation to second-line and third-line resolver groups. | | |
| **Minimum score to achieve this level:**     **'Y' for all mandatory ('M') questions** <br><br>                         **+   2 other 'Y'** <br><br> **answers** | | |

Copyright The Art of Service | Brisbane, Australia | Email: service@theartofservice.com
Web: http://theartofservice.com | eLearning: http://theartofservice.org | Phone: +61 (0)7 3252 2055

| Level 3 – Defined | Y | N |
|---|---|---|
| The definition of an Incident is clearly understood as distinct and separate from a Problem; this definition is applied consistently across the organization. | | M |
| All Incidents are assigned a priority according to a clearly defined and understood prioritization coding system based on impact and urgency. | | M |
| New Incidents are matched with previously detected incidents, problems or known errors. | | M |
| A number of Incident models have been defined and documented to provide a consistent approach for frequently recurring Incidents. | | M |
| Clear roles and responsibilities have been identified, defined, documented and appointed for the Incident Management process. | | M |
| All staff involved in incident management have access to relevant information such as known errors, problem resolutions and the configuration management system (CMS). | | M |
| Each support group has and follows clearly defined and documented procedures to manage incidents escalated to that group. | | |
| Ownership of an incident initiated from a user remains with the Service Desk, even when it has been escalated to a higher-level support group. | | |
| Where an immediate resolution is not known for unmatched incidents, clearly defined activities for investigation and diagnosis activities exist. | | |
| Prior to Incident closure, categorization codes are updated if the incident was initially categorized incorrectly. | | |

Copyright The Art of Service | Brisbane, Australia | Email: service@theartofservice.com
Web: http://theartofservice.com | eLearning: http://theartofservice.org | Phone: +61 (0)7 3252 2055

| | Y | N |
|---|---|---|
| There is a documented policy governing whether an incident can be reopened after its initial closure. | | |
| There is a consolidated system used to manage all incident records and the associated references to problems, known errors and change records. | | |
| Where an incident resolution requires a normal change, a Request for Change (RFC) is raised and subsequently handled by Change Management. | | |
| **Minimum score to achieve this level:**     **'Y' for all mandatory ('M') questions**<br><br>               **+    3 other 'Y'**<br><br>**answers** | | |

| Level 4 – Quantitatively Managed | Y | N |
|---|---|---|
| Relative standards and other quality criteria applicable for the registration of incidents and for call handling are made clear to the incident management team. | | M |
| The organization will set and review targets or objectives for incident management on a regular basis. | | M |
| Surveys are conducted to measure the user/customer satisfaction with the handling of incidents by the IT service provider. | | M |
| Incidents are tracked to ensure that resolution timeframes documented in SLAs are met, with any potential breaches being flagged and escalated to the appropriate party for resolution. | | |
| Reports are regularly produced that shows the percentage of incidents resolved at the first-line or second-line support groups. | | |

Copyright The Art of Service | Brisbane, Australia | Email: service@theartofservice.com
Web: http://theartofservice.com | eLearning: http://theartofservice.org | Phone: +61 (0)7 3252 2055

| | Y | N |
|---|---|---|
| The Incident Manager will review sample incident records to review compliance to the defined process/procedures and quality standards. | | |
| Trends in the workload of incident management is reported on and utilized to identify the staffing requirements for various work periods. | | |
| Actions are taken to identify and reduce the number of incidents from users that bypass the Service Desk or self-help system. | | |
| **Minimum score to achieve this level:** **'Y' for all mandatory ('M') questions**<br><br>**+    2 other 'Y'**<br><br>**answers** | | |

| Level 5 – Optimizing | Y | N |
|---|---|---|
| The costs of incidents are tracked; this information is included in assessing the Total Cost of Ownership of Services. | | M |
| Reviews seek to identify recurring incidents that could be resolved by the user themselves using self-help mechanisms. | | M |
| Incident Management provides evidence of incidents related to releases in order to better support future test designs and test models. | | |
| Incident Management provides data for process and service improvement initiatives. | | |
| Incident Management provides Incident reference information to Event Management for Event/Incident cross reference. This seeks to enhance the early detection and resolution of exceptions. | | |

Copyright The Art of Service | Brisbane, Australia | Email: service@theartofservice.com
Web: http://theartofservice.com | eLearning: http://theartofservice.org | Phone: +61 (0)7 3252 2055

| | |
|---|---|
| **Minimum score to achieve this level:**     'Y' for all mandatory ('M') questions<br><br>                                 +   1 other 'Y'<br><br>**answer** | |

Copyright The Art of Service | Brisbane, Australia | Email: service@theartofservice.com
Web: http://theartofservice.com | eLearning: http://theartofservice.org | Phone: +61 (0)7 3252 2055

## Problem Management

Problem Management is responsible for managing lifecycle of all problems. The primary objectives of Problem Management are:

- To prevent problems and resulting incidents from happening
- To eliminate recurring incidents
- To minimize the impact of incidents that cannot be prevented.

Clear distinction should be made between the purpose, scope and activities of Problem Management and those of Incident Management. In many cases staff may not clearly understand the distinction, and as a result not utilize their efforts in the most effective and efficient manner.

For most implementations of Problem Management the scope includes:

- The activities required to diagnose the root cause of incidents and to determine the resolution to those problems
- Activities that ensure that the resolution is implemented through the appropriate control procedures, usually through interfaces with Change Management and Release & Deployment Management
- Proactive activities that eliminate errors in the infrastructure before they result in incidents and impact on the business and end users.

Copyright The Art of Service | Brisbane, Australia | Email: service@theartofservice.com
Web: http://theartofservice.com | eLearning: http://theartofservice.org | Phone: +61 (0)7 3252 2055

| Level 1 – Performed (Ad-hoc) | Y | N |
|---|---|---|
| Problem records are logged and maintained for all identified problems. | | M |
| Problem Management exists as a consistent and repeatable process across our organization. | | M |
| There is a defined method for calculating incident priority that is based on the relative impact, costs to identify and fix the problem and whether there is an existing workaround. | | |
| Problem Management proactively manages Known Errors to aid Incident Management in the efficient resolution of related incident. | | |
| Problem Management submits an RFC to Change Management to remove a Known Error in the production environment. | | |
| **Minimum score to achieve this level:**     **'Y' for all mandatory ('M') questions**<br><br>        **+   1 other 'Y'**<br><br>**answer** | | |

| Level 2 – Managed | Y | N |
|---|---|---|
| There is a procedure or system for classifying problems, with a detailed set of categorization and prioritization codes. | | M |
| A database or ticketing system is maintained to record details for all identified problems and Known Errors. | | M |

Copyright The Art of Service │ Brisbane, Australia │ Email: service@theartofservice.com
Web: http://theartofservice.com │ eLearning: http://theartofservice.org │ Phone: +61 (0)7 3252 2055

| | | |
|---|---|---|
| Training or awareness sessions have been conducted or made available electronically for staff, providing guidelines and instructions for how to employ the Problem Management process. | | M |
| There are clear guidelines instructing staff about when and how a problem record should be created. | | M |
| Clear roles and responsibilities have been identified, defined, documented and appointed for the Problem Management process. | | M |
| There are guidelines that are defined to assist in the investigation and diagnosis of problems. | | |
| Time and resources are made available to focus on either Reactive or Proactive Problem Management. | | |
| A Problem Management process owner with accountability for the process across the organization has been appointed. | | |
| A policy exists that documents rules for accepting and managing Known Errors related to a release. | | |
| **Minimum score to achieve this level:** **'Y' for all mandatory ('M') questions** **+ 2 other 'Y' answers** | | |

Copyright The Art of Service │ Brisbane, Australia │ Email: service@theartofservice.com
Web: http://theartofservice.com │ eLearning: http://theartofservice.org │ Phone: +61 (0)7 3252 2055

| Level 3 – Defined | Y | N |
|---|---|---|
| A policy exists that documents when and how a problem record should be created and which roles can perform this action. | | M |
| Procedures define the steps to be taken for recording, classification, updating, escalation, resolution and closure of all problems | | M |
| Problem Management has a defined guidelines and procedures for both Reactive AND Proactive Problem Management | | M |
| There are documented guidelines to assist in evaluating whether an RFC should be raised to remove a Known Error. | | M |
| There are one or more defined and documented methodologies used for Problem Investigation (e.g. Kepner Tregoe, Pareto Analysis, Pain-Value Analysis etc.). | | M |
| There are effective mechanisms in place that ensure that the required stakeholders (various IT staff, teams and suppliers) are involved in Problem Management when required. | | M |
| There is a defined set of procedures and guidelines used to review Major Problems. | | |
| Ownership of an incident initiated from a user remains with the Service Desk, even when it has been escalated to a higher-level support group. | | |
| Problem Management provides feedback to Availability Management and Capacity Management for assisting in capacity planning or initiatives to improve availability. | | |
| Changes submitted by Problem Management document the resources required, risk and overall justification for the respective Change. | | |

Copyright The Art of Service | Brisbane, Australia | Email: service@theartofservice.com
Web: http://theartofservice.com | eLearning: http://theartofservice.org | Phone: +61 (0)7 3252 2055

| | Y | N |
|---|---|---|
| Problem Management uses information from the Configuration Management System (CMS) to assist in the investigation and resolution of problems. | | |
| SLAs are used to assist in the prioritization of problem records. | | |
| Time and resources are made available for the employment of both Reactive AND Proactive Problem Management. | | |
| There are defined guidelines used for the approval of workarounds before they are accepted into the Known Error Database or integrated ITSM tool. | | |
| There is a Problem category for managing any security issues. | | |
| **Minimum score to achieve this level:**     **'Y' for all mandatory ('M') questions** <br><br>                            **+   4 other 'Y'** <br><br> **answers** | | |

| Level 4 – Quantitatively Managed | Y | N |
|---|---|---|
| Relative standards and other quality criteria applicable for the registration of problem records and for the associated investigation are made clear to the problem management team. | | M |
| The organization will set and review targets or objectives for Problem Management on a regular basis. | | M |
| Regular metrics are produced showing how Problem Management is contributing to the prevention and efficient resolution of incidents. | | M |
| Problem and Known Error records are tracked to maintain an understanding of their progression and priority. | | |

Copyright The Art of Service | Brisbane, Australia | Email: service@theartofservice.com
Web: http://theartofservice.com | eLearning: http://theartofservice.org | Phone: +61 (0)7 3252 2055

| | | |
|---|---|---|
| Reports are regularly produced that shows the contribution of Proactive Problem Management, such as an overall decline in the number of incidents being reported. | | |
| The costs for Problem Management analysis and resolution activities are understood. | | |
| The Problem Manager will review sample problem and Known Error records to review compliance to the defined process/procedures and quality standards. | | |
| Trends in the workload of Problem Management is reported on and utilized to identify the staffing requirements for both Reactive AND Proactive Problem Management. | | |
| **Minimum score to achieve this level:**     **'Y' for all mandatory ('M') questions**<br><br>                                 **+    2 other 'Y'**<br><br>**answer** | | |

| Level 5 – Optimizing | Y | N |
|---|---|---|
| The costs of problems and Known Errors are tracked; this information is included in assessing the Total Cost of Ownership of Services. | | M |
| Reviews seek to improve the investigation and diagnosis methods used in determining the root-cause of the problem. | | M |
| Collaboration between Incident Management, Problem Management and Release & Deployment Management is facilitated to optimize improvements being made across the processes. | | |
| Problem Management provides data for process and service improvement initiatives. | | |

Copyright The Art of Service | Brisbane, Australia | Email: service@theartofservice.com
Web: http://theartofservice.com | eLearning: http://theartofservice.org | Phone: +61 (0)7 3252 2055

| | | |
|---|---|---|
| Event, Incident and Problem data is used for Proactive Problem Management. | | |
| Performance and demand of services and systems are enhanced using Problem Management data. | | |
| **Minimum score to achieve this level:**     **'Y' for all mandatory ('M') questions**<br><br>                       **+   2 other 'Y'**<br><br>**answer** | |

Copyright The Art of Service | Brisbane, Australia | Email: service@theartofservice.com
Web: http://theartofservice.com | eLearning: http://theartofservice.org | Phone: +61 (0)7 3252 2055

Request Fulfillment

Request Fulfillment is concerned with fulfilling requests from the end user community using consistent and repeatable methods. The objectives include:

- To provide a channel for users to request and receive standard services for which a pre-defined approval (from Change Management) qualification exists
- To provide information to users and customers about the availability of services and the procedure for obtaining them
- To source and deliver the components of requested standard services
- To assist with general information, complaints or comments.

The scope of Request Fulfillment is influenced heavily by the success of Change Management and what types of pre-approved changes can be effectively managed, controlled and implemented by the IT department. As part of continual improvement, the scope of Request Fulfillment should grow over time as maturity develops for Service Requests, including:

- Users and customers asking questions, providing comments and making complaints
- Users seeking changes to their access levels (utilizes Access Management)
- Users wishing to have common services and applications installed for their use.

Many elements of Request Fulfillment may be automated through the use of self-help such as websites and user applications, with manual activities being used where necessary to fulfill the request.

**Standard Change:** A pre-approved Change that is low risk, relatively common and follows a procedure or work instruction. There may still be authorization from other groups such as Human Resources; however Change Management will not need to approve each execution of the standard change.

Copyright The Art of Service | Brisbane, Australia | Email: service@theartofservice.com
Web: http://theartofservice.com | eLearning: http://theartofservice.org | Phone: +61 (0)7 3252 2055

| Level 1 – Performed (Ad-hoc) | Y | N |
|---|---|---|
| There is a repeatable and consistent process used for managing Service Requests from the end user community. | | M |
| There is a mechanism for recording and tracking Service Requests throughout their lifecycle. | | M |
| There is an agreed method for calculating the priority of the Service Request based on the relative business need, urgency and resources required for fulfillment. | | |
| There is at least some approval mechanism used to verify whether a Service Request should be fulfilled (e.g. financial, line management etc.) | | |
| The Request Fulfillment process is used to manage all user requests not relating to a service disruption (i.e. incident), including questions, complaints, hardware and application requests, and requests for modification of access. | | |
| **Minimum score to achieve this level:**     **'Y' for all mandatory ('M') questions** <br><br>              **+    1 other 'Y'** <br><br> **answer** | | |

| Level 2 – Managed | Y | N |
|---|---|---|
| There is a procedure or system for menu selection, allowing a user or Service Desk analyst to provide input for the request to be routed to the appropriate fulfillment team. | | M |

Copyright The Art of Service │ Brisbane, Australia│ Email: service@theartofservice.com
Web: http://theartofservice.com │ eLearning: http://theartofservice.org │ Phone: +61 (0)7 3252 2055

| | | |
|---|---|---|
| There is a set of documented procedures documenting how different Service Requests should be approved, escalated and fulfilled. | | M |
| Training or awareness sessions have been conducted or made available electronically for staff, providing guidelines and instructions for how to employ the Request Fulfillment process. | | M |
| There is a defined procedure for closing Service Requests. | | M |
| Clear roles and responsibilities have been identified, defined, documented and appointed for the Request Fulfillment process. | | M |
| SLAs are used to determine appropriate response and fulfillment timeframes. | | |
| Time and resources are made available for the appropriate engagement of Request Fulfillment. | | |
| A process owner with accountability for the process across the organization has been appointed. | | |
| Details of the various Service Requests that can be submitted are made available to customers and users. | | |
| **Minimum score to achieve this level:** **'Y' for all mandatory ('M') questions** **+ 2 other 'Y' answers** | | |

Copyright The Art of Service | Brisbane, Australia | Email: service@theartofservice.com
Web: http://theartofservice.com | eLearning: http://theartofservice.org | Phone: +61 (0)7 3252 2055

| Level 3 – Defined | Y | N |
|---|---|---|
| Documentation exists that states the goals, objectives and activities and procedures of the Request Fulfillment process. | | M |
| The Service Catalogue is used to define the outcomes for customers and users from which Service Requests are derived. | | M |
| There are a range of pre-defined Service Request models, that document the different steps to take for different types of requests (e.g. provisioning a desktop or provisioning standard applications). | | M |
| There are documented guidelines to assist in evaluating whether an RFC should be raised to in relation to the Service Request. | | M |
| There is a method for associating the relevant cost-centre for chargeback or accounting purposes. | | M |
| The Service Desk acts as the primary point of contact for all Service Requests, escalating them to other fulfillment teams when required. | | M |
| There is a procedure for raising a Service Request when necessary for resolution of an incident. | | |
| There is a survey mechanism that allows the user/customer to provide feedback (satisfaction level) about the Request Fulfillment process. | | |
| Release & Deployment makes pre-approved Release Packages available to be provisioned by Request Fulfillment. | | |
| The Configuration Management System is updated accordingly throughout the fulfillment of a Service Request. | | |
| When a Service Request relates to the provision of applications, checks are made to ensure there is sufficient availability of software licenses. | | |

Copyright The Art of Service | Brisbane, Australia | Email: service@theartofservice.com
Web: http://theartofservice.com | eLearning: http://theartofservice.org | Phone: +61 (0)7 3252 2055

| | | |
|---|---|---|
| Change Management regularly provides new and updated Standard Changes to be handled as a Service Request. | | |
| There is a range of self-help available to users (e.g. via the internet or intranet) that enables the user to log and/or view Service Requests. | | |
| There are a number of pre-defined workflows built into the ITSM tool used to manage Service Requests, automating parts or all of the fulfillment process. | | |
| Service Level Agreements clearly define the expected fulfillment timeframes for different Service Requests. | | |
| Request Fulfillment is appropriately integrated with Access Management to ensure the Information Security Policy is enforced. | | |
| **Minimum score to achieve this level:**    **'Y' for all mandatory ('M') questions**<br><br>                 **+    5 other 'Y'**<br><br>**answers** | | |

Copyright The Art of Service | Brisbane, Australia | Email: service@theartofservice.com
Web: http://theartofservice.com | eLearning: http://theartofservice.org | Phone: +61 (0)7 3252 2055

| Level 4 – Quantitatively Managed | Y | N |
|---|---|---|
| Relative standards and other quality criteria applicable for the registration of Service Requests and any follow-up actions is documented and made available for all teams. | | M |
| The organization will set and review performance targets or objectives for Request Fulfillment on a regular basis. | | M |
| Regular surveys are conducted to measure the customer and user satisfaction of the Request Fulfillment Process. | | M |
| Regular reports are used to understand the volume of different types of Service Requests. | | |
| Reports are regularly produced that shows the utilization of self-help for Request Fulfillment. | | |
| The cost of provisioning each type of Service Request is understood. | | |
| The Request Fulfillment Manager will review sample Service Request records to review compliance to the defined process/procedures and quality standards. | | |
| Trends in the workload of Request Fulfillment is reported on and utilized to identify the future staffing requirements. | | |
| **Minimum score to achieve this level:** **'Y' for all mandatory ('M') questions**<br><br>**+ 2 other 'Y'**<br><br>**answer** | | |

| Level 5 – Optimizing | Y | N |
|---|---|---|

Copyright The Art of Service | Brisbane, Australia | Email: service@theartofservice.com
Web: http://theartofservice.com | eLearning: http://theartofservice.org | Phone: +61 (0)7 3252 2055

| | |
|---|---|
| The costs of managing Service Requests are tracked; this information is included in assessing the Total Cost of Ownership of Services. | M |
| Reviews seek to improve the most frequently occurring Service Requests by making self-help available to users and building automation into the process workflow. | M |
| Feedback from Service Level Management is used to improve the Request Fulfillment process from the customer perspective. | |
| Request Fulfillment provides data for process and service improvement initiatives. | |
| Reviews are held with Change Management to review the list of standard changes; adding, changing or removing items as appropriate. | |
| Request Fulfillment provides input into the development of a service solution, so that the capabilities to make requests associated with the service are built-in. | |
| **Minimum score to achieve this level:** **'Y' for all mandatory ('M') questions** **+ 2 other 'Y'** **answer** | |

Copyright The Art of Service │ Brisbane, Australia │ Email: service@theartofservice.com
Web: http://theartofservice.com │ eLearning: http://theartofservice.org │ Phone: +61 (0)7 3252 2055

## Access Management

Access Management's primary objective is to provide capabilities for the granting of authorized users the right to use a service while preventing access to non-authorized users. In doing so, it helps to protect the confidentiality, integrity and availability (CIA) of the organization's services, assets, facilities and information.

Access Management is the operational execution of the policies, rules, processes and architectures implemented by Information Security and Availability Management within the Service Design phase. Although in many cases it is a process that is typically coordinated by the Service Desk, it can involve many different internal and external groups responsible for Service Operations.

Access Management ensures that users are given the right to use a service, but it does not ensure that this access is available at all agreed times – this is provided by Availability Management. As described above, the process is often centrally coordinated by the Service Desk (being the single point of contact with the end user community), but can involve the Technical and Application Management functions. Where access is controlled by external suppliers, interfaces need to be developed to coordinate requests for/modifications to access levels.

Copyright The Art of Service | Brisbane, Australia | Email: service@theartofservice.com
Web: http://theartofservice.com | eLearning: http://theartofservice.org | Phone: +61 (0)7 3252 2055

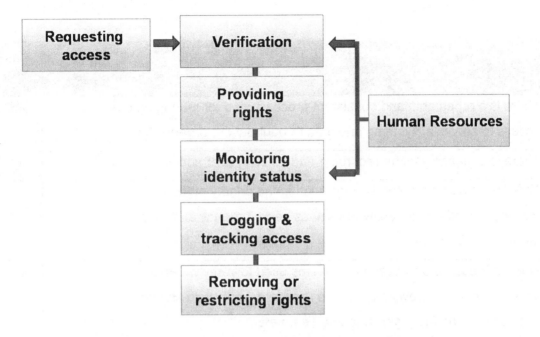

**Figure: Typical Activities of Access Management**

Copyright The Art of Service | Brisbane, Australia | Email: service@theartofservice.com
Web: http://theartofservice.com | eLearning: http://theartofservice.org | Phone: +61 (0)7 3252 2055

| Level 1 – Performed (Ad-hoc) | Y | N |
|---|---|---|
| There is a repeatable and consistent process used for managing user access to services, systems and data throughout the organization. | | M |
| There is a mechanism for recording and tracking user access events. | | M |
| There is an agreed method for calculating the priority of the Service Request based on the relative business need, urgency and resources required for fulfillment. | | |
| There are agreed approval mechanisms used to verify whether access should be provisioned to the user (e.g. verify with Human Resources, Line Manager, Security Team etc.) | | |
| Access Management uses the Information Security Policy to reduce any confusion regarding the process. | | |
| **Minimum score to achieve this level:**　　**'Y' for all mandatory ('M') questions**　　　　　　　　　　**+　1 other 'Y'** **answer** | | |

| Level 2 – Managed | Y | N |
|---|---|---|
| There is an approved information security policy that is communicated to all relevant IT personnel, customers and users. | | M |
| Requests are generated by normal Human Resources (HR) processes. This occurs when staff are hired, promoted, moved, transferred or when they leave the organization. | | M |

Copyright The Art of Service │ Brisbane, Australia │ Email: service@theartofservice.com
Web: http://theartofservice.com │ eLearning: http://theartofservice.org │ Phone: +61 (0)7 3252 2055

| | | |
|---|---|---|
| Training or awareness sessions have been conducted or made available electronically for staff, providing guidelines and instructions for how to employ the Access Management process. | | M |
| There are supporting tools that enable staff to monitor the users' identity status, provide or restrict rights and log user access events. | | M |
| Clear roles and responsibilities have been identified, defined, documented and appointed for the Access Management process. | | M |
| SLAs are used to determine appropriate timeframes and communication to be conducted when managing user access requests. | | |
| Time and resources are made available for the appropriate execution of Access Management. | | |
| Mechanisms exist to ensure all staff hires, moves or retirements trigger the execution of Access Management. | | |
| All exceptions or deviations from the Information Security Policy are logged and notified to the appropriate team/individuals. | | |
| All security breaches or identified weaknesses are logged, with follow-up action taken by the appropriate team/individuals. | | |
| **Minimum score to achieve this level:** **'Y' for all mandatory ('M') questions** **+ 2 other 'Y' answers** | | |

Copyright The Art of Service | Brisbane, Australia | Email: service@theartofservice.com
Web: http://theartofservice.com | eLearning: http://theartofservice.org | Phone: +61 (0)7 3252 2055

| Level 3 – Defined | Y | N |
|---|---|---|
| Documentation exists that states the goals, objectives, activities and procedures of the Access Management process. | | M |
| The impact of changes on security controls are assessed before changes are implemented. | | M |
| Arrangements that involve external organizations having access to information systems and services based on a formal agreement that defines all necessary security requirements. | | M |
| All security controls used in the production environment are documented. | | M |
| There is a method for associating the relevant cost-centre for managing access requests (if required by Financial Management). | | M |
| The Service Desk contributes to Access Management by providing an accessible channel to make access requests and by communicating any changes of the Information Security Policies to the user community. | | M |
| There is a procedure/system defined to check for and resolve role conflicts when provisioning access. | | |
| All security incidents are reported and recorded in line with the incident management procedure as soon as possible. | | |
| The Configuration Management System is updated accordingly if rights and access is changed. | | |
| When an access request relates to the provision of applications, checks are made to ensure there is sufficient availability of software licenses. | | |

Copyright The Art of Service │ Brisbane, Australia │ Email: service@theartofservice.com
Web: http://theartofservice.com │ eLearning: http://theartofservice.org │ Phone: +61 (0)7 3252 2055

| | | |
|---|---|---|
| Audits are performed on a regular basis to identify exceptions, comparing the actual rights provisioned to the documented rights and privileges (e.g. provided by HR). | | |
| A procedure exists for handling situations where a user is under investigation (e.g. for breach of policy) but still requires some access. | | |
| Department managers, HR staff and other relevant stakeholders have been provided education or training on how to engage with the Access Management process. | | |
| Service Level Agreements clearly define the expected fulfillment timeframes for different access requests/activities. | | |
| Request Fulfillment is appropriately integrated with Access Management to ensure the Information Security Policy is enforced. | | |
| **Minimum score to achieve this level:**     **'Y' for all mandatory ('M') questions** <br>                   **+   4 other 'Y'** <br> **answers** | | |

Copyright The Art of Service | Brisbane, Australia | Email: service@theartofservice.com
Web: http://theartofservice.com | eLearning: http://theartofservice.org | Phone: +61 (0)7 3252 2055

| Level 4 – Quantitatively Managed | Y | N |
|---|---|---|
| Relative standards and other quality criteria applicable for the notes and documentation created within the Access Management process. | | M |
| The organization will set and review targets or objectives for Access Management on a regular basis. | | M |
| Regular metrics are produced showing how Access Management is ensuring compliance to the Information Security Management policy. | | M |
| Mechanisms are in place to enable the types, volumes and impacts of security incidents and malfunctions to be quantified and monitored. | | |
| Regular reports are produced to communicate the number and types of exceptions found when auditing access rights. | | |
| The percentage of requests grouped by method of submission (e.g. using self-help, via the Service Desk, direct requests from management etc.) are monitored and reported. | | |
| The operational costs associated with Access Management have been quantified. | | |
| Measurements of user and customer satisfaction with the Access Management process are taken and reviewed. | | |
| Performance measures such as the time taken to provide, restrict and remove rights are reviewed and reported. | | |
| **Minimum score to achieve this level:** **'Y' for all mandatory ('M') questions** **+ 3 other 'Y' answer** | | |

Copyright The Art of Service │ Brisbane, Australia│ Email: service@theartofservice.com
Web: http://theartofservice.com │ eLearning: http://theartofservice.org │ Phone: +61 (0)7 3252 2055

| Level 5 – Optimizing | Y | N |
|---|---|---|
| The costs of managing access and rights for services are tracked; this information is included in assessing the Total Cost of Ownership of Services. | | M |
| Reviews seek to improve the most frequently occurring Service Requests by making self-help available to users and building automation into the process workflow. | | M |
| Access Management provides input to Availability Management in the design of security systems, controls and infrastructure. | | M |
| Feedback from Service Level Management is used to improve the Access Management process from the customer perspective. | | |
| Access Management provides data for process and service improvement initiatives. | | |
| Reviews are held with Information Security Management to embed short-term and long-term improvements to the Information Security Policy. | | |
| Request Fulfillment provides input into the development of a service solution, so that the capabilities to make requests associated with the service are built-in. | | |
| **Minimum score to achieve this level:** **'Y' for all mandatory ('M') questions** <br><br> **+ 2 other 'Y'** <br><br> **answer** | | |

Copyright The Art of Service | Brisbane, Australia | Email: service@theartofservice.com
Web: http://theartofservice.com | eLearning: http://theartofservice.org | Phone: +61 (0)7 3252 2055

## FURTHER READING

For more information on other products available from The Art of Service, you can visit our website: http://www.theartofservice.com

If you found this guide helpful, you can find more publications from The Art of Service at: http://www.amazon.com

Copyright The Art of Service | Brisbane, Australia | Email: service@theartofservice.com
Web: http://theartofservice.com | eLearning: http://theartofservice.org | Phone: +61 (0)7 3252 2055

# 5 Index

Copyright The Art of Service | Brisbane, Australia| Email: service@theartofservice.com
Web: http://theartofservice.com | eLearning: http://theartofservice.org | Phone: +61 (0)7 3252 2055

Copyright The Art of Service | Brisbane, Australia | Email: service@theartofservice.com
Web: http://theartofservice.com | eLearning: http://theartofservice.org | Phone: +61 (0)7 3252 2055

Copyright The Art of Service │ Brisbane, Australia │ Email: service@theartofservice.com
Web: http://theartofservice.com │ eLearning: http://theartofservice.org │ Phone: +61 (0)7 3252 2055

passwords  65, 107

payments  69-70, 79-80, 83

performance  23, 26, 72, 75-7, 87-8, 124, 132, 152

personnel  10, 43, 72, 78, 81, 162

plan  25, 35-6, 81, 83

policies  38, 64, 109-10, 127, 141, 148-9, 160, 165

Policy Statement  38, 110-11

Problem Management  40, 54-5, 66, 95, 146-7, 149-51

problem records  147-50

problems  27, 31, 53-5, 57, 60-1, 66, 87, 110, 118, 122, 134, 142-3, 146-51

process owner  44, 52, 137, 155

processes  14, 18, 38-44, 51-2, 56, 58, 62-3, 95, 115, 124-9, 131, 139-41, 147-8, 151,
     159-60, 162

products  31-2, 168


R


reader  35, 38, 50, 68, 91-2, 105, 110, 117

regeneration  77

registration  57, 92-3, 136, 143, 150, 158

regulations  75, 78

Request Fulfillment  153, 155-9, 165, 167

resolution  21, 36, 53, 136, 142-3, 146, 149-50, 156

resources  4, 6-7, 15, 18, 22, 24, 55, 59, 62, 120, 125, 127, 148-50, 154-5, 162-3

responsibilities  4, 15, 18-20, 27, 41, 47, 57, 71, 122, 134-5, 141-2, 148, 155, 163

review  2, 34, 36-7, 39, 45-6, 49, 67, 89-90, 98, 104, 109, 116, 159

RFC (Request for Change)  21, 58, 92, 143, 149, 156

rights  70, 163-7

ROI (Return on Investment)  108

roles  4-5, 18-21, 24, 29, 36, 45, 47, 134, 139, 141, 149


S


scope  3, 30, 35, 39, 41, 46, 51, 76-8, 109-10, 115, 132, 146

self-help  140, 153, 157-9, 166-7

Service Asset & Configuration Management  56, 66

Service Continuity Management  42, 62, 108

Service Desk  3, 5-11, 13-16, 18-23, 34-7, 40-2, 45-9, 87-8, 90-3, 95, 97, 104-9, 113,
     115-17, 119-21, 139-40

service improvement initiatives  137, 144, 151, 159, 167

Service Level Agreements  139, 141, 157, 165

Service Level Management  52, 59, 61, 159, 167

Service Management  18, 23, 51, 123, 131-2

service provision  6, 66, 93, 113

service quality  66, 131, 139

Copyright The Art of Service | Brisbane, Australia | Email: service@theartofservice.com
Web: http://theartofservice.com | eLearning: http://theartofservice.org | Phone: +61 (0)7 3252 2055

Service Requests   20-1, 36, 92, 124, 134, 139, 153-9, 162, 167
skills   4, 14, 16, 46, 78
SLAs (Service Level Agreement)   23, 52, 55, 62, 64, 135-6, 139, 141, 143, 150, 155, 157, 163, 165
software   37, 44, 56, 59, 70, 72, 75-7, 84
staff   4, 9, 11, 15-16, 21-2, 27, 43-4, 46-7, 51, 63, 72, 89, 92, 122, 148-9, 162-3
systems   27, 30-2, 37, 44-5, 53, 60, 70, 77, 81, 92, 124, 134, 140, 147, 152, 154

## T

Technical Management   3, 5, 24-6
technology   5, 8, 10, 14, 24, 26, 30-1, 131
termination   70, 73-4, 79-82
thresholds   133-4
tickets   53-5, 63
tool   30, 44, 46-7, 50-4, 56-64, 97, 163
Total Cost of Ownership of Services   144, 151, 159, 167

## U

user community   5-6, 8, 139, 153-4, 160, 164
users   5, 8, 10, 13, 15, 20-1, 40, 53, 59, 63, 87-8, 144, 153-7, 159-60, 162-3, 165-7

## V

vendor   46, 64-5
version   34, 49, 67, 87, 90, 98, 104, 109, 116, 123-4
Virtual Service Desk   10

## W

warnings   52-3, 60-1, 132, 135
warranties   77-80
workarounds   12, 147, 150

Copyright The Art of Service | Brisbane, Australia | Email: service@theartofservice.com
Web: http://theartofservice.com | eLearning: http://theartofservice.org | Phone: +61 (0)7 3252 2055

Lightning Source UK Ltd.
Milton Keynes UK
UKOW022321081012

200237UK00003B/25/P